m_s

Who's Buri
Your F

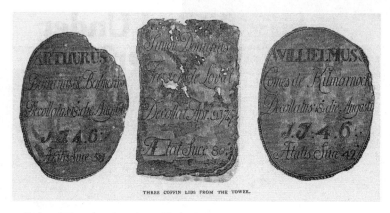
THREE COFFIN LIDS FROM THE TOWER.

Other Books by Geoffrey Abbott

Who's Buried Under Your Fl💀💀r?

London's Forgotten Cemeteries and Plague-Pits

Geoffrey Abbott

Yeoman Warder (retd),
HM Tower of London
Member of The Sovereign's Bodyguard of
the Yeomen of the Guard Extraordinary

**ERIC DOBBY
PUBLISHING**

First published in Great Britain 2007 by

Eric Dobby Publishing Ltd
Random Acres,
Slip Mill Lane
Hawkhurst
Cranbrook
Kent TN18 5AD

The right of the author to be identified as the Author of this work has been asserted by him in accordance with the Copyright, Designs and Patents Act 1988

ISBN 10: 1-85882-063-4
ISBN 13: 978-1-85882-063-7

Printed by Loupe Solutions

CONTENTS

Illustrations

With thanks to Christopher Holmes of Christopher
Holmes Photography, Kendal, Cumbria, for assistance
with the illustrative material.

FOREWORD

The National Gallery with St Martin's Church

F ew of those people visiting the bookshops along
Charing Cross Road or the National Gallery are
aware that somewhere beneath their feet lie the
remains of Charles II's mistress Nell Gwynne, notorious
criminal Jack Sheppard, and hundreds of others, buried
in the once-extensive cemetery of nearby St Martin's in
the Fields Church, Trafalgar Square; pet owners walking
their dogs across the playing fields of Vincent Square,
Westminster, would no doubt be similarly surprised if
they knew that the turf was laid over what was the burial
site of 1,200 Scottish prisoners and their wives, as would
commuters waiting for trains in Cannon Street Station;
they may complain about the lack of porters and are
completely oblivious of the skeleton staff beneath the
platforms, for the station was built on the site of the
cemetery of St John's Church, Cloak Lane. A length of

Shaftsbury Avenue covers part of Soho's St Annes' Church graveyard, in which no fewer than 110,240 corpses were laid to rest, one of them being that of Theodore, King of Corsica, interred in 1756, while people passing Charterhouse Square, Clerkenwell, could have no idea that 50,000 bodies were buried there in 20 years, the nearby Pardon Churchyard being the last resting place of those who had committed suicide or had died on the gallows.

Such consequences are inevitable, given that over the centuries countless millions of people have lived and died in London, some by natural causes, others by epidemics such as cholera, the Black Death and the Plague. Most of them were buried in the City's cemeteries, pest-fields and plague-pits; for instance, by 1889 there were 247,000 corpses buried in one grave yard, the City of London and Tower Hamlets Cemetery, 155,000 in Brompton Cemetery; 30,000 in Whitfield's Tabernacle Burial Ground, Tottenham Court Road, and 50,000 in Deptford Cemetery.

Much of this historic, if gruesome, information came to light when, in the early 1880s, a truly remarkable Victorian lady named Mrs Basil Holmes happened to be studying a map of London made by John Rocque between the years 1742-5, and she realised that many burial grounds and churchyards marked on it no longer existed. She listed them and after some research, the authorities included her findings in the *First Annual Report of the Metropolitan Public Gardens Association* in 1884, some ancient burial grounds having been converted to that use.

Encouraged by such recognition of her efforts, she proceeded to investigate all the London burial grounds of which she had found any record. She delved through hundreds of reports and Orders in Council, none of them comprehensive, among them being returns such as Places of Burial belonging to each *Parish or Precinct under the Authority of the Bishop of London, 1833* and *Places of Burial belonging to Dissenting Congregations within the Bills of Mortality*, returns which also included

VIEW OF THE CRYPT ON THE SITE OF THE LATE COLLEGE OF S.ᵗ MARTIN LE GRAND.
Discovered in clearing for the New Post Office

The Crypt of St Martin le Grand in 1818

the annual number of burials within them. So incomplete
the returns, so inaccurate the maps, that she decided to
visit each of the 364 sites personally and assess its size
and condition – or indeed whether there were any traces
at all of its original function – no mean feat for a Victorian
lady whose role in contemporary society certainly did
not include that of being a private detective or forensic
investigator! Her findings, written in her own inimitable
style, were published in 1901 in a book entitled *London's
Burial Grounds*, a condensed version of which follows,
together with information gleaned from other sources,
printed in the Appendices.

Since her book was written, the inevitable expansion of
London's population, the devastation caused by wartime
bombing, and urban modernisation, have resulted in
many, if not most of the sites she describes being further
replaced by housing estates and office blocks – and is that
where YOU now live or work? If so – who's buried under
YOUR floor?

CHAPTER ONE

MRS HOLMES' INTRODUCTION

Sheep in the Savoy Churchyard about 1825

I found many maps and books to be of use, but as it is never safe to take anything on trust, nothing but actual perambulations and inquiries on the spot could show the present size and condition of the 364 burial grounds I had discovered, and even several that are marked on the ordnance maps have been built upon since they were published, as, for instance, the German ground in the Savoy (the Strand), the additional ground to St Martin's in the Fields, and Thomas' ground in Golden Lane, Clerkenwell, all of which have disappeared.

I have had some curious experiences while graveyard-hunting. At first I was less bold than I am now, and was hardly prepared to walk straight into private yards and look round them until asked my business and driven to retire. 'My business' it is best not to reveal ordinarily. If one mentions that one is looking at a place because it was once a burial-ground, the fact will generally be denied, sometimes in good faith. But it is not unusual for an employee innocently to acknowledge that there are bones under the ground on which he is standing, whereas his master, if he knew of it, would be very angry. For it must be remembered that it is to the interest of the owner of a yard to keep the circumstance of its having been used for interments in the background, and he is not pleased if, when he wants to put up a wall or enlarge a shed, he is stopped from doing so by the enforcement of the *Disused Burial Grounds Act* of 1884 as amended by the *Open Spaces Act* of 1887.

I inquired of an old man once, in a court in Shoreditch, whether he remembered a graveyard existing by the workhouse."No," he said. I noticed a newer part of the building, evidently a recently erected wing, and asked him how long it had been built. "Oh, I moind," said he "when they was buildin' that, they carted away a ton of bones." Here was the evidence I was seeking.

It is often necessary, in order to see a grave-yard, to go into one of the surrounding houses and ask for permission to look out from a back window. Such permission is sometimes refused at once, sometimes it is most kindly given. I remember arousing a divided opinion upon this matter by knocking at the door of one of the upper rooms in the almshouses in Bath Street (St Luke's, EC1). I wanted to see the ground used as a garden by the inmates of the St Luke's Lunatic Asylum in Old Street, and which was at one time a pauper burial-ground for the parish. The old man did not at all like me invading his room, but the old lady was most affable, and had much to say upon the subject. At any rate I saw what I wanted, and made my mental report, but I left the old man grumbling at my unnecessary intrusion, and the old lady in smiles. I hope she did not suffer for her kindness. If one asks to go into a burial-ground it is usually imagined that one wants to see a particular grave. I have been supposed to have 'some one lyin' there' in all quarters of the metropolis, and in all sorts of funny little places. I have been hailed as a sister by the quietest of Quakeresses and the darkest of bewigged Jewesses, by the leanest and most clean-shaven of ritualistic Priests and by the bearded and buxom Dissenter. I remember, however, knocking at the gate of one Jewish ground which the caretaker was unwilling to let me enter. She asked me the direct question "Are you a Jewess?" I had to say no, but happily I was armed with the name of a gentleman who had kindly told me to mention it in any such difficulty. I answered, and I was allowed in. One day I climbed a high, rickety fence in a builder's yard in Wandsworth in order to see over the wall into the Friends' burial-ground. No doubt the men in the place thought me mad – anyway, they left me in peace.

I have often been assured that there is no possibility of a particular graveyard ever becoming a public garden by those who live, at a low rent, in the neighbouring cottage, on condition that they keep watch over the ground. Alas, before many months are over, they find that wires have been pulled somehow or other, and their precious yard is no longer available for their fowls to run in or for their clothes to dry in, but is invaded by their neighbours and their neighbour's unwelcome children. "They, the authorities, come four times a year to clear away the weeds" – that is the sort of caretaking that some burial-grounds are subjected to; and on the other 361 days in the year, all sorts of rubbish is deposited in them.

Twice I have had mud thrown at me, once by a woman in Cable Street E., and once by a man in Silchester Road, W., but these were wholly unprovoked attacks, in fact were accidental occurrences. For my general experience has been one of the greatest consideration and politeness. I have never been out of my way for the sake of idle curiosity, but have not hesitated to go down any street or court or to knock at any door which was in my way, and I have never had cause to regret it. An appearance of utter insignificance and an air of knowing where you are going and what you want, is a passport to all parts of London; and I have seen young men and maidens, one moment indulging in the roughest play, the next moment step off the pavement to let me pass. The clergy and others always seem to think their own people the very worst. "You don't know what this neighbourhood is like," I have heard over and over again, and I am thankful I don't. But as far as a superficial knowledge of the streets goes, they seem to be all much the same, and their frequenters too. To the children, at any rate, one never need to mind speaking. Poor little souls; they say "Miss," or "Mum," or "Missus," or "Teacher," or "Lady," but they never answer rudely. Even grave diggers and gardeners in cemeteries are generally communicative people who do not mind stopping their work for a bit and enlarging on the number of funerals etc. which they daily witness.

It is interesting to trace on maps of different dates, the rise and fall of a graveyard. First there is the actual field, which on some particular day, was acquired for the purpose. Then there is the burial ground formed and in use. Then the plot appears to be vacant – put to no purpose, or used as a yard. Lastly buildings are on it, and the graveyard has quite disappeared. One difficulty to be encountered needs much study to overcome; it is the different names by which the same ground is called in different books or plans. For instance, Chadwick mentions in his list one called St. John's, Borough, whereas the proper name for this same ground is Butler's burial-ground, Horselydown. As another instance, and there are scores, it may be mentioned that the Peel Grove burial-ground was called in some returns the North-east London Cemetery, in others Cambridge Heath burial-ground, and in others Keldy's ground.

Since 1883, as complete a list as I could make of the London burial-grounds has appeared in the *Reports of*

Peel Grove Burial-Ground, Bethnal Green

the Metropolitan Public Gardens Association, and I have, from time to time, been asked for information about the more obscure ones. In the summer of 1894 the London County Council instructed its Park Committee to make a return of all burial-grounds in the County of London, with their size, ownership and condition. Having been applied to for information and assistance, I offered to undertake the work. It involved some additional research at the British Museum, and a fresh perambulation. The offer being accepted, I commenced the task in February 1895 and sent in the return in June, accompanied by 60 sheets of the Ordnance Survey (25 inches to the mile) upon which the grounds were marked in colours, viz. those still in use blue, disused green, those converted into public recreation grounds green with a red border. I gave the number existing in the County and City of London as 362 of which 42 were still in use and 90 were public gardens and playgrounds. This did not include churches and chapels with vaults under them but without graveyards.

The cemeteries in the county do not represent all the parochial ones. There are, for instance, those of St George's, Hanover Square, and Kensington at Hanwell, the Paddington Cemetery in Kilburn, the Jewish at Willesden, and very many more just outside the boundary, not to speak of a large number in 'London over the Border', which to all extent is still London, although separated by the River Lea and governed by the West Ham Corporation.

The kindly notice taken of the return, which was published by the Council in October 1895, has encouraged me to prepare the present volume, in which there is scope for a general view of the subject, for further historical details, and for particulars of those grounds which no longer exist.

The more public interest is brought to bear upon the burial grounds, the more likely it is that they will be preserved from encroachments. The London County Council has special powers to put into force the provisions of the *Disused Burial Grounds Act*, and it has the record of their actual sites on the plans prepared by me. It is for the public to see that these provisions are carried out, not only for historical, sentimental, and sanitary reasons, but also because each burial-ground that is curtailed or annihilated means the loss of another space which may one day be available for public recreation; and considering that land, even in the poorest part of Whitechapel, fetches about £30,000 per acre, it is easily understood of what inestimable value is a plot of land which cannot be built on.

CHAPTER 2

THE GRAVEYARDS
OF PRIORIES AND
CONVENTS

Many monastic and conventual buildings in London had their own church or chapel. Some of these brotherhoods were small, and they may not have had burial-places of their own. In other cases burials may have taken place in the priory churches, which were always sought after for the purpose by outsiders, or in the cloisters. But most of the conventual establishments had a cemetery of considerable size, the 'cloister garth'.

When, after the Great Fire of London of 1666, the rubble of a demolished building which belonged to the Black Friars was cleared away, four heads in pots or cases of 'fine pewter', as reported by historian John Strype (1643-1737), were found in a cupboard in one of the walls. They were embalmed or preserved, and had tonsured hair. He imagined that they were the heads of 'some zealous priests or friars, executed for treason........ or for denying the King's Supremacy, and here privately deposited by the Black Friars.' It is possible that these heads were afterwards bought and taken to the Continent to be exhibited as holy relics (see Appendix D).

Recent discoveries have shown that the priory cloister of the Augustine Friars was immediately to the north-east of the Dutch Church in Austin Friars. St James's Priory, the Hermitage in the Wall, had a graveyard under the wall, on the other side of which was, and is, the churchyard of St Giles', Cripplegate. Huge warehouses and offices now cover its site. The burial-ground of the Priory of St Thomas Acon, in Ironmonger Lane, where pilgrims were buried who died on their visits to the chapel in honour of Becket, has also disappeared; but that of the priory of St Augustine Papey survives in the little churchyard of St Martin Outwich in Camomile Street, which was presented to the parish by Robert Hyde in 1558, while the nuns of St Helens were probably buried in what is now St Helen's Churchyard, Bishopgate Street, which used to be, according to the historian John Snow, much larger.

No trace is left of the burial places of the monks of Elsing Spital, the Crutched Friars, or the White Friars, or of that of the splendid priory and sanctuary of St Martin le Grand; they have gone with the buildings, of which only slight traces remain here and there, such as the porch of St Alphege, London Wall, which belonged to Elsing Spital Priory. Probably they all had burial-grounds within their precincts.

The crypt of St Martin's was opened out in 1818 and a very perfect stone coffin was found in it when the present Post Office Buildings in Foster Lane were erected. The churches themselves were always much resorted to as places of interment by those who were not connected with the priories, especially the four magnificent churches, all of which are now gone, of the Greyfriars, the Whitefriars, the Blackfriars and the Augustine Friars. The Dutch Church is the successor to the nave of the last-named. The site of the Greyfriars church is occupied by the present church and churchyard of Christ Church, Newgate Street. Here were buried Margaret, second wife of Edward I, Isabella, widow of Edward II, Joan Makepeace, wife of David Bruce, King of Scotland, and Isabella, wife of Lord Fitzwalter, the Queen of Man, besides the hearts of Edward II and Queen Eleanor, wife of Henry III, and, according to Weever 'the bodies of four duchesses, four countesses, one duke, twenty-eight barons and some thirty-five knights'; in all, six hundred and sixty-three persons of quality.

St. Katherine's Docks

Other principal convents and priories outside the City have also gone. The site of St Katherine's is buried in the dock of that name (see Supplement, Appendix D), and that of St John the Baptist's, Holywell (by Curtain Street, Shoreditch) has also gone.

The Churchyards of St Mary, Bromley, and St Saviour, Southwark, are the survivals of the conventual burying-places; the cemetery of the nuns at Bromley was on the south side of the church, and upon its site Sir John Jacob built the Manor House, the bones being put under the house. But about two years later, in 1813, the greater part of this site was again added to the churchyard, and re-consecrated.

The burial-ground of Westminster Convent, with the Abbot's garden, have given place to the district and market of Covent Garden (the latter now replaced by a shopping centre and tourist attractions). The houses in White Lion Street and Spital Square are on the site of the cemetery or garth of St Mary Spital. Here, after it ceased to be used for interments and before it was built upon, Spital Square was an open plot of ground with a pulpit in it and a house for the accommodation of the Lord Mayor

The Burial-ground of St Mary Rounceval Convent – now
Northumberland Ave – 1896

and Corporation when they came on their annual visit to
hear the 'Spital Sermon'.

The Nuns' burial-ground at Clerkenwell, and part of
the beautiful cloister, existed until about one hundred
years ago in the garden of the Duke of Newcastle's
house, and its site is now occupied by the houses on
the west side of St James' Walk, a little north-east of St
James' Church. The Convent of St Mary Rounceval was
superceded by Northumberland House, subsequently
pulled down when Northumberland Avenue was
made; and the churchyard of Holy Trinity, Minories, in
Whitechapel – now merely part of the road – may be a
relic of the Nunnery of the Minoresses of St Clare. The
Cistercian abbey of St Mary of Grace and the Carthusian
priory of the Salutation were built on plague burial
grounds; the former has disappeared under the site of
the Royal Mint, Tower Hill (see Appendix D), the latter
survives in the Charterhouse.

On the north side of King Street, Hammersmith, just
east of the Broadway Station, is the large red building

Ruins of the Convent of St Clare

The Royal Mint 1895 – Built on the site of the Cemetery of
the Convent of St Mary at Grace and an earlier Pest Field

known as the Convent of the Sacred Heart. Brewer, in his *Beauties of London and Middlesex* published in 1816, thus describes the burial ground of this convent 'The grave stones are laid flat on the turf, and the sisters are placed, as usual, with their feet to the east, the priests alone having the head towards the altar.' Cardinal Manning disposed of this little cemetery, which was by the lane on the east side, when erecting the present building. "It was dug up and done away with," according to one of the sisters at present in the convent. But two similar burial-grounds are still to be found in this immediate neighbourhood; one is disused, the other is still in use. The former is behind the Convent of the Good Shepherd in Fulham Palace Road, only about 14 by 12 yards in size, and closed a few years ago. The latter is at the extreme end of the garden of Nazareth Home in Hammersmith Road, under the wall of Great Church Lane. It is even smaller than the one in Fulham Palace Road, and has been in use for upwards of forty years, but as only the sisters are interred here, it would appear to be still available for about another twenty years. The graves are in neat rows, a small cross on each, with the name, or adopted name, of the sister whose body lies beneath. It forms a little enclosure in the large space and garden behind the buildings of the Home, where many children are taught and many old people live. Another enclosure contains their poultry, and another, a cow. The whole establishment is very interesting, and not the least interesting part of it is this little cemetery, of the existence of which, in all probability, very few of the inhabitants of the surrounding streets have any knowledge.

I have visited one other convent burial-ground, and in each case it is necessary to go through the ceremony of being peeped at through a grating and, when admitted, passed along corridors and through rooms while the doors are locked behind, and only granted permission to see what I want after some time of waiting and a large amount of explanation. I have since been told that I was singularly favoured by being admitted into the Franciscan Convent of Portobello Road, where the Mother Superior herself most kindly took me to see the little cemetery. It is a charming little corner of a very pretty garden, a triangular grass plot edged with trees, not above about a quarter of an acre in extent. It was formed in 1862 and first used in 1870, only five burials taking place in twenty-three years. It is, of course, merely for the interment of the nuns who, having given up the world and shut themselves into the convent, find their last resting place within its precincts.

CHAPTER 3

ST PAUL'S, THE TOWER AND THE CITY CHURCHYARDS

Tower of London: Site of the Scaffold with the Chapel of St Peter

St Paul's Cathedral Churchyard extended, especially on its northern side, farther than it does now, part of it being known as 'Pardon Church Yard'. In 1549 the cloister, the chapel, the charnel house and the tombs were all cleared away by the Protector Somerset, the

Tower of London: Interior of St Peter Chapel

materials being used for his new mansion in the Strand, and the bones from the charnel house – Stow says one thousand cartloads – were reinterred in Finsbury Field.

At the Tower there were four recognised burial-places; the churchyard of St Peter ad Vincula, the vaults beneath the Church, the vaults 'behind the church', and the outer graveyard. The last named was a narrow strip by the eastern wall, probably used for the burial of the humbler members of the numerous households which composed the Tower precinct. This ground was demolished when the Tower Bridge was built in 1896, the land being required for the wide approach thereto (see Appendix D). The Chapel itself is not as beautiful as it might be, and the graveyard attached to it is little more than a part of the Tower courtyard, but the sad memories connected with it will always hallow this spot. (see Appendix D).

In the quaint little church of Holy Trinity, supposed to be a survival of the Minoresses of St Clare in the Minories, there is still shown what is said to be the head of the Duke of Suffolk, the father of Lady Jane Grey. It is in a glass case,

The Church of Allhallows the Great in 1784

preserved like leather, some hairs clinging to the scalp, while the false (badly aimed) blow of the executioner can clearly be seen just above the place where the head was severed from the trunk. The verger keeps this marvellous relic locked up in a pew (see Supplement, Appendix D). As for the churchyard of Allhallows' Barking, by the Tower, it has lately been entirely covered with building materials owing to the restoration of the church; it was, according to Stow 'sometime far larger.' (For a burial on Tower Hill, see Appendix D).

The City of London, as we know it now, averages, roughly speaking, a mile and a half from east to west, and three quarters of a mile from north to south. Its highways represent untold wealth, and its byways reek with poverty and dirt. It contains the most bustling thoroughfares and the most retired quarters; it is full of business and affairs up to date, yet is teeming with antiquarian interest and relics of ancient history. So the City churches, with their old-world churchyards, are wedged in between huge modern warehouses, offices and public buildings, churchyards sometimes so entirely detached from churches, always pressed upon by houses, so small, so rank, so forgotten. Thus we hear of an injunction being sought for, to restrain the would-be reformer (developer) from cutting off a two-foot-wide strip behind the houses in Crooked Lane; and the Commissioners of Sewage possess the right, and sometimes use it, of curtailing a churchyard in order to widen a road. In 1884 for instance, they gave £750 for a piece at the eastern end of Allhallows' Churchyard, London Wall. The remainder of that little ground is now a public garden, laid out in 1894 by the Metropolitan Gardens Association, a quiet resting-place in the busy thoroughfare, with a piece of the ancient City wall still existing in it.

Most of the churchyards entirely detached from churches are the sites of the burned buildings which were used as burial-grounds by the amalgamated parishes – for the mournful calamity of 1666, the Great Fire of London, visited the churches with peculiar severity, 89 of them being destroyed, 51 being re-built by Wren and his followers, and 35 of which were not replaced. The site of Allhallows' the Great, Upper Thames Street, was recently sold to a brewery company, but has not yet been built on, because it is thought that an injunction will be served upon the builder and that it will be made a test case. One of the oldest churches founded in the City is sometimes supposed to be that of St Mary Woolnoth, Lombard Street, and is presently threatened by a railway company.

The churchyard of St Olave's, Hart Street, is an interesting one; the old gate has skulls and cross-bones on it, and in this ground were interred a vast number of the victims of the Plague of 1665, which is said to have originated in this parish in the nearby Drapers' Almhouses (see Appendix D). There were four churches in the City dedicated to St Botolph, a pious Saxon who built a monastery in Lincolnshire in AD 654. The churchyards of all four are now public gardens – St Botolph's, Bishopgate; St Botolph's Aldgate; St Botolph's, Aldersgate, and St

Botolph's, Billingsgate. The last-named church was not rebuilt after the Great Fire, and the site of one of its churchyards is now occupied by a new warehouse with red heads on the frontage, on the south side of Lower Thames Street. What remains of the other part of it is a small three-cornered asphalted court, open to the public, with seats, a drinking fountain and a coffee stall.

A melancholy incident took place in the Aldgate churchyard here in September 1838 when two men, a gravedigger and a fish-dealer, lost their lives in a grave by being poisoned with the foul air. The grave was a 'common one', such as was often kept open for two months until filled with seventeen or eighteen bodies. It may safely be said that all the City burial-grounds were crowded to excess. Their limited area would invite such treatment, and it was only natural that the City parishioner should choose to be interred in the parish churchyard, unless the still greater privilege were afforded him to being buried in the vaults under the church.

Most of the remaining City churchyards are quiet little spaces, surrounded by huge warehouses. Many are only approached through the churches, and are invisible from the road. St Mildred's in Bread Street is, unfortunately, used as a store-yard for ladders of all sizes, while the very small piece that remains by the tower of St Mary Somerset, Thames Street, is full of old iron. One or two are private gardens, such as St Michael's Churchyard, Queenhithe; others have been paved and added to the public footway, such as that of St Mary Abchurch, their extent being still visible.

This is the case with the churchyard of St Michael Bassishaw in Basinghall Street. The ground is now part of the pavement, but the two large trees which grew in it are still flourishing. The untidy little yard in Farringdon Street, which is used as a volunteer drill-ground, was once an additional burying-place for St Bride's, Fleet Street. It was given to the parish by the Earl of Dorset, on condition that no more burials should take place in the southern part of the churchyard which was opposite his house. The house was destroyed in the Great Fire and the churchyard was used again. The grave-yard of St Christopher le Stocks is the garden of the Bank of England, and the author John Timbs states that, although he does not vouch for the authenticity of the story, the mound for the burial-ground of Whitfield's Tabernacle in Tottenham Court Road was brought from this churchyard 'by which the consecration fees were saved' (because it had already been consecrated!).

Of the City churchyards which have been completely annihilated, apart from other kinds of burial-grounds within this area, there must have been at least forty. And this destruction has been due to the dissolution of the priories, the formation of new streets, and the invasion of the railways. Three churches in Farringdon Ward Within have gone, St Ewans, south of Newgate Street, St Genyn within St Martin le Grand, and St Nicholas in the Fleshambles, Newgate Street (see Appendix D).

When Queen Victoria Street was made, the churchyards of St Mary Mounthaw, St Nicholas Olave, and St Mary Magdalen, Knightrider Street, disappeared. That of St Michael, Crooked Lane, a plot given by one Robert Marsh and consecrated in 1392, was sacrificed for King William Street, and that of St Benet, Paul's Wharf – now the Welsh Church – where Inigo Jones was buried, for St Benet's Hill. A complete list of them will be found in the Appendices.

Cannon Street Station of the South Eastern Railway covers the churchyard of St Mary Bothaw; and for Cannon Street Station of the District Railway, that of St John's, Cloak Lane, was destroyed, the human remains being 'dug up, sifted, put in chests with charcoal, nailed down, put one on top of the other in a brick vault and sealed up forever – or rather till some others in turn come to turn them out again.' Part of the General Post Office is on the churchyard of St Leonard, Foster Lane; the Mercer's Hall is on that of St Thomas Acons, where the pilgrims are buried; the Mansion House Station is on that of Holy Trinity the Less; and the Mansion House itself is on that of St Mary Woolchurch Haw, in which a balance used to stand 'for weighing the wool.'

In 1668 the Lord Mayor 'issued out a Precept commanding, among other wholesome orders ....that the Inhabitants, Householders, and others concerned, should not throw or suffer any Ashes, Dirt, or other Filth, to be cast out before any Church or Churchyard, upon pain of 20 shillings.' But now, in 1896, we need visit very few of these same churchyards before we come to one in which rubbish of all kinds is allowed to accumulate and remain. Yet they are sacred spots, consecrated ecclesiastically and historically, and instead of being permitted to sink into the oblivion of insignificance, they should be made beautiful in memory of the dead and for the benefit of the living, for in them are 'the tombs of the wealthy and the humble heaps of the poor.'

And it may be interesting here to give particulars of a case in which the decision arrived at is valuable to those who are fighting the battle of protection. In 1881 the London School Board introduced a Bill for the purpose of acquiring compulsory powers over the burial-ground in Bream's Buildings, Fetter Lane, belonging to the church of St Dunstan in the West and which adjoins the Greystoke Place Board School. The rector and churchwardens entered an opposition to the Bill and appeared before the Committee of the House of Lords and were successful, the School Board being given merely the right of way to the school through the graveyard.

CHAPTER 4

CHURCHYARDS OUTSIDE THE CITY

Our London churchyards of today were once village churchyards and were attached to quiet old churches which, with a few neighbouring houses, stood far away from the town and were encircled with fields. There are many now living who can remember walking from the City to St Mary's, Islington, by a footpath through the meadows, and such was also at one time the case with Paddington, St Pancras, Hackney, Shoreditch, Stepney, Bow, Bromley, Rotherhithe, Lewisham and many other parishes. It is difficult to realise it now, and yet it is only in the present century that they have been merged into the great metropolis, and separated by many miles of houses from the hedges and fields.

And it is also a fact that many wells, conduits and pumps in and around London were – and some still are – not only in close proximity to the churchyards, but actually in them. The water from St Clement's Well and St Giles' Well came through the burial-grounds. The site of the Bride's Well, which gave its name to the precinct and the hospital, is still marked by the pump in an alcove of the wall of St Bride's Churchyard in Fleet Street. There was a pump by St Michael le Querne and one in the churchyard of St Mary le Bow, against the west wall of the church. There was a well in the crypt of St Peter's, Walworth, a pump in Stepney Churchyard, and another in St George's in the East, Limehouse, to which his parishioners used to resort for drinking water until the Rev. Harry Jones, during a cholera scare, hung a large placard on it with the words – 'Dead Men's Broth!' And Charles Dickens used to picture the departed, when he heard the churchyard pumps at work, as saying "Let us lie here in peace; don't suck us up and drink us!"

Nordern's plan and later ones gives us a picture of the remoteness of the outer parishes. Here is his description of old St Pancras Churchyard 'It standeth all alone, as utterly forsaken, old and weather-beaten; about this church have bin many buildings, now decayed, leaving poor Pancras without companie or comfort, yet it is now and then visited with those from Kentishtowne and Highgate, which are members thereof. When there is a corpse to be interred, they are forced to leave it within this forsaken church or church-yard, where no doubt it resteth as secure against the day of resurrection as if it lae in stately St Paules.' It would indeed be curious to see what Nordern would think now of this churchyard, with the Midland Railway trains unceasingly rushing across it, and the 'dome' and 'trophy' of headstones numbering four hundred and ninety-six, not to speak of the stacks and walls of them round about, which were moved into one part of the ground when the other part – Catholic Pancras – was acquired by the railway company. Poor Pancras is not forsaken now, it is in the midst of streets and houses, and what remains of the churchyard is full of seats and people. This particular ground, with many others in the same neighbourhood, were famed later on as the scenes of the operations of body-snatchers, the first indictment for body-stealing taking place at St George the Martyr ground – behind the Foundling hospital – in 1777 (*see* my *Grave Disturbances* – the story of the body-snatchers). But it must be remembered that, although one time body-snatchers or resurrection men carried on a brisk trade, yet where one body may have been disinterred for hospital use, one hundred were removed to make room for others.

The largest of the churchyards are Stepney, Hackney and Camberwell. That of St Anne's, Limehouse, had a strip taken off it in 1800, when Commercial Road was made; that of St Paul's, Hammersmith, was similarly curtailed in 1884. The present churches of Hammersmith and Kensington are far larger than their predecessors, and therefore the churchyards dwindled when they were built. St Clement Danes and St John's, Westminster, once stood in fair-sized churchyards; now, in each case, there is only a railed-in enclosure round the church.

But one of the most serious shortenings was at St Martin in the Fields. In fact, of those buried from this particular parish, few can have been un-disturbed, except, perhaps, in the cemetery in Pratt Street, Camden Town, now a public garden, which belongs to St Martin's. One of the parochial burial-grounds is under the northern block of the buildings forming the National Gallery, another one is lost under Charing Cross Road, while a third one, now a little garden, in Drury Lane, was so disgustingly overcrowded that no burials could take place there without the disturbance of other bodies, which were crowded into pits dug in the ground and covered with boards. But to return to the churchyard itself, the burial-ground immediately surrounding the church, where Nell Gwynne, mistress of Charles II, and Jack Sheppard, the notorious criminal who was hanged at Tyburn in 1724, were buried (see Appendix D). A strip on the north side and a piece at the east end still exist, flagged with stones, and were planted with trees, provided with seats, and opened to the public in 1887. But once there was a large piece of ground to the south side, where now there is none, called the Waterman's Churchyard. Its disappearance is accounted for by the following inscription on a tablet on the church wall; 'These catacombs were constructed at the expense of the Commission of Her Majesty's Woods and Forests, in exchange for part of the burial-ground of this parish, on the south side of the church, given up for public improvements, and were consecrated by the Lord Bishop of London on 7th day of June, 1831.'

In the Sunday Times of 12 June 1831, these vaults are thus described; 'The new vaults under St Martin's burying ground are the most capacious structure of the sort in London. They were opened on Tuesday, at the consecration of the new burial-ground. They consist of a series of vaults, running out of each other in various directions; they are lofty, and when lighted up, as on Tuesday, really present something of a comfortable appearance.' After relating some details about the size and number of arches, the quantity of coffins they would hold, etc., the description closes with these words 'Crowds of ladies perambulated the vaults for some time, and the whole had more the appearance of a fashionable promenade than a grim depository of decomposing mortality.'

This account reminds me very much of the ceremony which took place after the opening of St Peter's Churchyard, Walworth, as a garden, in May 1895. The Rector had kindly provided tea in the crypt, a huge space under the church where gymnastic and other classes are held. This crypt used to be full of coffins lying about at random, with a well in the centre, but a faculty was obtained for their removal to a cemetery. The scene on the day to which I refer was a very gay one. Where, a few months previously, there had been coffins and dirt, there was a well white-washed building, lighted by plenty of gas, lace curtains between the solid pillars and low arches, a number of little tables with tea, cakes etc. and many brightly-attired girls to wait on the visitors, who enjoyed their refreshment to the enlivening strains of a piano.

The churchyard of St Giles in the Fields is a very interesting one. It might well now be called St Giles in the Slums, although of late years the surrounding streets have been much improved and the worst courts cleared away. Before there was a church of St Giles there was a lazaretto or leper hospital on the spot, and what is now the churchyard was the burial-ground attached thereto. It holds many centuries of the dead, and was frequently enlarged, Brown's Gardens being added in 1628, until the parish secured an additional burial-ground in 1803, adjoining that of St Pancras. It is related in Thornbury's *Haunted London* that in 1670 the sexton agreed to furnish the rector and churchwardens with two fat capons, ready dressed, every Tuesday se'night in return for being allowed to introduce certain windows into the churchyard side of his house. But it could not have been a pleasant churchyard to look at. It was always damp, and vast numbers of the poor Irish were buried in it (the ground had originally been consecrated by a Roman Catholic), and it is hardly to be wondered at, that the parish of St Giles enjoys the honour of having started the Plague of 1665. And the practices of body-snatching carried on there at the beginning of this century were equal to the worst anywhere – revolting ill-treatment of the dead was the daily custom. In contrast, from a dramatic point of view, the burial-ground attached to St Paul's, Covent Garden, is most interesting, as it contains the graves of a large number of actors.

By the close of the last century and at the beginning of this one, the want of additional burial space was much felt in several parishes. Some had 'poor grounds' and some, like St James's, Clerkenwell, had a 'middle ground', this being now the playground of the Bowling Green Board School, but the extra graveyards were all small and all crowded. Many of the district churches, built at the commencement of the present century, also had churchyards attached. In Bethnal Green, for instance, not only is there the burial-ground of St Matthew's, which was consecrated in 1746 and has vaults under the school as well as the church, but there are those of St Peter's, St Bartholomew's and St James' the Less, the first two being laid out as gardens, and the last being a dreary, swampy waste containing about ten sad-looking tombstones and a colony of cocks and hens.

It is impossible to touch upon all the churchyards outside the City, but I must refer briefly to the four principal parish churches which have disappeared. The present building of St Mary le Strand only dates from 1717; the original one stood 'in a fair cemetery' much nearer the river, but the church and churchyard disappeared to make room for Somerset House; the Church of St John the Evangelist,

St. Matthew's, Bethnal Green, 1818

Tybourn, was removed in 1400 and the first church of St Marylebone was built to take its place. Provision was made for the preservation of the churchyard, but it also disappeared before long. It was near the site of the present Court-house in Stratford Place, under which bones were dug up in 1727 and 1822. Tybourn Church was removed because it was in too lonely a situation, and yet so near the main road from Oxford to London, that robbers and thieves were always breaking into it to steal the bells, images, ornaments, etc.

The Church of St Margaret, Southwark, stood in the middle of the Borough High Street, with a much used graveyard round it, which was enlarged in 1537. But it was so inconvenient a place, and the ground was so much used for holding markets in, that it was removed about 1600. The old town hall took the place of the church, and the Borough Market is still held on or near the site of the churchyard.

When St Katherine's Docks were made, in 1827, St Katherine's Church, the ruins of the hospital (dating from 1148), two churchyards of considerable size, and the

St. Katherine's Hospital - The Brothers' Houses in 1781

whole parish – inns, streets, houses and all, were totally annihilated (see Appendix D). The whole establishment was, to a certain extent, rebuilt near Regent's Park. It is said that a quantity of human remains from the churchyard were used to fill up some old reservoirs, etc., in the neighbourhood; but, at any rate, it is a fact that they were distributed among the East-end churchyards, and several cartloads were taken to Bethnal Green and deposited in St Matthew's ground, where the slope up to the west door of the church is composed of those bodies from St Katherine's. There were originally steps leading to the entrance, but the steps are buried under this artificial hill, the ground having been raised several inches.

CHAPTER 5

PESTFIELDS AND PLAGUE PITS

The Pest-houses in Tothill Fields

Considering that we have records of the visitation of London by direful plagues and pestilencies at frequent intervals during ten centuries, and that these visitations always led to a mortality far in excess of the ordinary one, it is not to be wondered at that from time to time, special burial-places had to be provided to meet the special need.

In early days the visitations (epidemics) were so ordinary that when mentioned in the histories of London, they are not taken much account of. Here is one record: 'The plague making its appearance in France in 1361, the king, to guard against the contagion spreading in London, ordered that all cattle for the use of the City should be slaughtered, either at Stratford on one side of the town, or at Knightsbridge at the other side, to keep the air free from filthy and putrid smells' (these were assumed to be the source of the disease). This regulation was certainly wholesome, but the close dwellings of which the City then consisted, were always fit receptacles for contagious dis-orders; the plague accordingly came over and in two days destroyed 1,200 persons.

In 1349 two large tracts of land were set aside for the interment of those who then died of the plague, Noorhouck writing a concise account; 'at length a great pestilence reached London, where the common cemeteries were not capacious enough to receive the vast number of bodies, so that several well-disposed persons were induced to purchase ground to supply (remedy) that defect. Amongst the rest, Ralph Stratford, Bishop of London, bought a piece of land called No-Man's-Land, which he inclosed with a brick wall, and dedicated it to the burial of the dead. It was three acres in extent and was afterwards known as Pardon Churchyard, Pardon Street (EC1), being used for the interment of executed people and suicides. Wilderness Row, now merged into Clerkenwell Road, marks its site.

Adjoining to this was a place called Spittle Croft, the property of St Bartholomew's Hospital, Clerkenwell, containing thirteen acres and a rod of ground, which was purchased for the same use of burying the dead, by Sir Walter Manny, and was long remembered by an inscription fixed on a stone cross upon the premises, the translation from the Latin inscription being 'A great plague raging in the year of our Lord 1349, this burial ground was consecrated, wherein, and within the bounds of the present monastery, were buried more than 50,000 bodies of the dead, many others thereforward to the present time; whose souls the Lord have mercy upon. Amen.'

On this ground the Charterhouse now stands, while the gardens and courts of the Charterhouse, the Square, the site of a demolished burial-ground for the pensioners – Sutton's Ground – and the burial-ground which still exists at the north end of the precincts, are all part of the Spittle Croft and of the monastery burial-ground. There have been many attempts to do away with the Charterhouse, to substitute streets and houses for the old buildings, gardens and courts, but happily it is not so easy as it once was to tamper with land consecrated for burials, even though that land may have been set aside 550 years ago.

There was also another piece of ground purchased at the east end of the City, just without the wall, by John Corey, a clergyman, for the same use; on which spot was afterwards, in this same reign, founded the Abbey of St Mary of Grace, for Cistercian monks; it is now covered by the Victualling Office and adjoining houses. It was asserted that not one in ten escaped this calamity, and that not less than 100,000 persons died in the whole. The Victualling Office was where the Royal Mint at present stands, on Tower Hill, and if one may trust William Newton's plan, the abbey graveyard was where the entrance courtyard is now (the Royal Mint buildings, north-east of the Tower of London, have now been converted into private residences; see Appendix D).

The numbers who died in subsequent visitations must have helped not a little to fill the parish churchyards, but it was not until the year of the Great Plague, 1665, that there seems to have been any very general provision of extra ground, although the pest-house ground in the Irish Field near Old Street, was consecrated in 1662, especially for the parish of St Giles, Cripplegate. But the plague of 1665 taxed the resources of the Mayor, magistrates, and citizens of London in a manner that was unprecedented. All through that fateful summer and autumn, and on into the commencement of the following year, did it play havoc with the people. In August and September it was at its height. The exact number of persons who died could not be known, for thousands of deaths were never recorded. Bodies were collected by the dead-carts, which were filled and emptied and filled again from sunset to dawn, and no account was kept of the numbers thrown into the pits. At any rate, between August 6th and October 10th, 49,605 deaths were registered in the Bills of Mortality as from the Plague, and Daniel Defoe, whose *Journal of the Plague Year* gives every detail that any one can wish for, considered that during the visitation, at least 100,000 must have perished, in addition to those who wandered away with the disease upon them, and died in the outlying districts. 'The number of these people were great. The country people would go and dig a hole at a distance from them, and then, with long poles and hooks at the end of them, drag the bodies into these pits, and then throw the earth in from as far as they could cast it, to cover them. It is pretty certain that many unrecorded burials took place in fields of Stoke Newington.'

London must have been a sad sight. All shows, pleasures and pastimes were stopped; people crowded continually into the churches; huge fires were always kept burning in the streets (to cleanse the 'poisonous air'), children were kept out of the churchyards to stop the disease from spreading, the city was cleared of all 'hogs, dogs, cats, tame pigeons and conies'; special dog-killers were employed, and food and assistance were given to the needy, while those who could afford to, fled into the country.

The plague, introduced from Holland, first broke out in Long Acre and gradually spread all over London. When it became impossible to bury in the ordinary way, huge pits were dug in the churchyards and bodies were deposited in them without coffins. The chief plague pit in Aldgate Church-yard was about 40 ft. long, 15 or 16 ft. broad, and 20 ft. deep, and between the 6th and the 20th of September, 1,114 bodies were thrown into it. But it soon became necessary to make new burial-grounds and new pits for the reception of the dead, as the common graves of every parish became full.

There were pest-houses in the ground to the north of Old Street and in Tothill Fields, Westminster, to which infected persons were taken. They corresponded to the isolation hospitals of today. But they could only accommodate, at the most, 300 patients or so, and were wholly inadequate to meet the need. The pest-houses in Old Street, or rather Bath Street, St Luke's, were long ago destroyed; Pest House Row and Russell Row used to mark their sites. But a portion of the pest-field exists in the garden behind St Luke's Lunatic Asylum, which was used as a burial-ground for the parish of St Giles, Cripplegate, until the formation, in 1732, of St Luke's 'poor ground.' The pest-houses in Tothill Fields were standing at the commencement of the present century. They were known as the 'five houses' or the 'seven chimneys' and were erected in 1642. The Tothill Fields, no longer being needed as a plague burial-ground, were sub-sequently built upon, but not until they had been used for the burial of 1,200 Scotch military prisoners with their wives. A considerable portion of the fields is, however, still open, and is known as Vincent Square, Westminster, the playground of the Westminster Schoolboys. Mackenzie Walcott, in his *Memorials of Westminster*, states that Harding's stoneyard in Earl Street, is the site of the principal plague-pit. This, I believe, is now the yard of Her Majesty's Stationery Office, Waste Paper Department.

Defoe gives a very careful description of some of the plague-pits and burial-grounds which were made in his immediate neighbourhood. He mentions;

'1. A piece of land beyond Goswell Road, near Mount Mill, where abundance were buried promiscuously from the Parishes of Aldersgate, Clerkenwell, and even out of the City. This ground, as I take it, was since made a Physick Garden, and after that, has been built on.' Mount Mill was on the north side of Seward Street.

2. A piece of ground just over the Black Ditch, as it was called, at the end of Holloway Lane in Shoreditch Parish; it has since been made a yard for keeping Hogs and for other ordinary uses, but is quite out

of Use for a burying-ground.' This Holywell Mount burial-ground has been 'in use' again since Defoe's time, and was also used as a plague-pit before 1665. Originally the site of a theatre dating from the time of Shakespeare. and named after the neighbouring Holywell Convent in King John's Court, it afterwards became a burial-ground famous as being used for the interment of a great many actors. There is a small part of it left, but at the outside not more than a quarter of an acre. It is behind the church of St James', Curtain Road, and is approached by a passage from Holywell Row. A parish room has been built on it, and what remains is used as a timber yard. The piece between the parish room and the church is bare and untidy.

3. The third place mentioned by Defoe was 'at the Upper end of Hand Alley in Bishopsgate Street, which was then a green field, and was taken in particularly for Bishopsgate Parish, tho' many of the Carts out of the City brought their dead thither also, particularly out of the Parish of Allhallows on the Wall.'

He then goes on to describe how this place was very soon built on, though the bodies were, in many cases, still undecomposed, and he states that the remains of 2,000 persons were put into a pit and railed round in an adjoining passage. New Street, Bishopsgate Street, now occupies the site of Hand Alley.

Besides this there is a piece of land in Moorfields, etc. Here he refers to the Bethlem burial-ground, which was not made at that time, but enlarged. Defoe finally mentions the extra grounds which had to be supplied to Stepney, then a very large extended parish. They included a piece of ground adjoining the churchyard, which was afterwards added to it; and in 1886, in laying out this churchyard as a public garden, some human remains, without coffins, and very close to the surface, were accidentally disturbed at the south-western end of the ground.

Another of the Stepney pest-grounds was in Spital-fields 'where since a chapel or Tabernacle has been built for ease to this great parish.' I believe it to be St Mary, Spital Square. Another was in Petticoat Lane. 'There were no less than five other grounds made use of for the Parish of Stepney at that time, one where now stands the Parish Church of St Paul's, Shadwell, and the other where now stands the Parish Church of St John at Wapping.' The churchyards of these two churches, the former of which is a public garden, and the latter of which is still closed, are therefore survivals of pest-fields.

But there are three other places to account for which Defoe does not localise. One was possibly in Gower's Walk, Whitechapel, where human remains, without coffins, were come upon recently in digging the foundations for Messrs. Kinloch's new buildings. The remains were removed in boxes to a railway arch in Battersea in the winter of 1893-4. I saw this excavation myself, the layer of black earth, intermingled with bones, being between two layers of excellent gravel soil.

One additional ground bought at the time of the Plague was on the north side of Mile End Road. By about 1745 it was used as a market garden, and now the site is occupied by houses south of the junction of Lisbon and Collingwood Streets, Cambridge Road. Besides these it is certain that a large tract of land south of the London Hospital was also used for interments, and the Brewer's Garden and the site of St Philip's church were probably parts of this ground, which is known as Stepney Mount. On the north side of Corporation Row, Clerkenwell, in digging for foundations for workmen's dwellings, a number of human remains were found. This site may have been a plague-pit, or it may have been a burial-ground for an old Bridewell nearby, or an overflow from a graveyard in Bowling-green Lane.

The chief place for interment for those who died of the plague in Southwark was the burial-ground in Deadman's Place, now called Park Street. Here vast numbers of bodies were buried. The graveyard was afterwards attached to an Independent Chapel, and many eminent Dissenters were buried there, for it soon became a sort of Bunhill

Fields for South London. Now the carts, the trucks and the barrels of Messrs. Barclay and Perkins' Brewery roll on rails over the remains of the victims of the plague and the Dissenting ministers with their flocks.

But pest-fields were needed in the west of London as well as in the north, south, and east, and in addition to Tothill fields there was a large tract of land set aside near Poland Street, upon the site of which the St James's Workhouse was subsequently built, a piece of the ground surviving still in the workhouse garden. Carnaby Street and Marshall Street, Soho, were also built on the site about the year 1723, when three acres, known as Upton Farm, were given in exchange in the fields of Baynard's Watering Place, Bayswater, upon which Craven Hill Gardens now stands. There was a plague-pit near Golden Square, Soho, this district being all a part of the pest-field at one time.

The orchard of Normand house, by Lillie Road, Fulham, is said, by Mrs S C Hall, to have been filled with bodies in the year of the Great Plague. The site of the orchard has almost gone; Lintaine Grove and the houses on the north side of Lillie road were built upon it. There is still a piece vacant and for sale, at the corner of Tilton Street, Fulham, about three-quarters of an acre in extent. Knightsbridge Green, opposite Tattershalls, was also used for the victims of the Plague, and those who died in the Lazar Hospital.

There used to be an additional burial-ground for Aldgate parish in Cartwright Street, E., consecrated in 1615. This, at the beginning of this century, was covered with small houses, and on part of the site the Weigh House School was built in 1846. The rookery (slum) was cleared by the Metropolitan Board of Works nearly forty years later, when Darby Street was made, and the vacant land was offered as a site for workmen's dwellings. I brought the case to the notice of the Metropolitan Public Gardens Association and the Board was communicated with. At first it was denied that any part of the site had been a burial-ground, but excavations were made and human remains were found. Nor was this really necessary, for the workmen who had pulled down the houses, and the authorities at the school, were well aware of the fact, and knew of actual tomb-stones being unearthed, upon which a date as late as 1806 had been found. The Board of Works caused the plans for the surrounding new buildings to be altered, and what is left of the site of the burial-ground is now an asphalted playground adjoining the southern block. A certain gentleman afterwards wrote and circulated a pamphlet in which he stated that the Metropolitan Board of Works had discovered one of the sites set apart in Whitechapel for a pest-ground in 1349, whereas the fact was that the Board had been driven, somewhat against its will, to preserve, as an open space, the site of a consecrated burial-ground belonging to the parish of St Botolph, Aldgate. That it may once have been a part of a pest-field is likely enough, for they abounded in the district, but the age of the Aldgate ground was, I consider, sufficient to account for the driest of dry bones found there.

Although the Plague has not re-appeared, there have been periods of great mortality from other diseases. Special provisions for burial had to be made at the time of the cholera visitations. In the outbreak in 1832, 196 bodies were interred in a plot of ground adjoining the additional burial-ground for Whitechapel, now the playground of the Davenant Schools. A large piece of ground by the churchyard of All Saints, Poplar, on the north side of the Rectory, was also used for the purpose, and the circumstance is recorded on the monument which stands in the middle of it.

The fact that the bodies in the pest-fields and plague-pits were usually buried without coffins, and were only wrapped in rugs, sheets, etc., has accelerated their decay, and it can no longer be thought dangerous when such pits are opened. Not that I wish, in any way, to defend the disturbance of human remains, for I hold that no ground in which interments have taken place should be used for any other purpose than that of an open space, and apart from the legal and sentimental aspects of the question, human remains, in whatever state of decay they may be, are not fit foundations for buildings, nor is it seemly or proper to gather them up and burn them in a hole, or to cram them casually into chests or 'black boxes,' to be padlocked and deposited in other grounds or convenient vaults. But the old plague-pits, the very crowded churchyards, and the private grounds where the soil was saturated with quicklime, the coffins smashed at once, and decay in every way hurried, are likely now to be less insalubrious than those grounds where lead and oaken coffins – specially intended to last for generations (see Appendix D) – are still in good preservation, and only occasionally give way and let out the putrifactive emanations.

CHAPTER 6

THE DISSENTERS' BURIAL GROUNDS

Foremost among the burial-grounds devoted especially to Dissenters (Nonconformists) is Bunhill Fields – not the New Bunhill Fields in Newington, nor Little Bunhill Fields in Islington, nor the City Bunhill Ground in Golden Lane, nor the Quakers' ground in Bunhill Row – but the real, genuine, original Bunhill Fields, City Road.

The land on the north side of the City and south of Old Street was variously called the Moorfields, Finsbury Fields, the Artillery Ground, Windmill Hill, and Bone-Hill or Bon-hill. In the year 1549, when the Charnel Chapel in St Paul's Churchyard was pulled down 'the bones of the dead, couched up in a charnel under the chapel, were conveyed from thence into Finsbury Field, by report of him who paid for the carriage thereof, amounting to more than one thousand cart-loads, and there laid on a moorish ground, which, in a short time after, being raised by the soilage of the City, was able to bear three windmills.' The number of windmills was later on increased to five, and they may be seen on many old maps of London. Heretics used to be interred in Moorfields, and bones from St Matthew's, Friday Street, were moved to Haggerston; in fact many acres in this district were in use for the purpose of burying in.

The land north of the Artillery Ground was known as Bonhill or Bunhill Field 'part whereof, at present denominated Tindal's or the Dissenters' great Burial-ground was, by the Mayor and Citizens of London, in the year 1665, set apart and consecrated as a common Cemetery, for the interment of such corps as could not have room in their parochial burial-grounds in that dreadful year of pestilence. However, it is not being made use of on that occasion, the said Tindal took a lease thereof, and converted it into a Burial-ground for the use of Dissenters.'

So wrote Maitland in 1756, but before that time a large plot was added on the north, and eventually the whole cemetery measured about five acres. There, at least 100,000 persons found their last resting-place, including vast numbers of Methodists, Baptists, Presbyterian and Independent ministers. The ground belongs to the Corporation; it is not laid out as a garden, but paths have been made and seats placed in it, the gates being open during the day.

On the south side of the Thames the largest and most important of the Dissenters' burial-grounds was that attached to the Independent Chapel in Deadman's Place, now called Park Street, Southwark, originally a plague-ground, and very much used for the burial of victims. Here, many more ministers were buried, whose names are household words wherever Dissenters are gathered together. If the mantle of Bunhill Fields has fallen anywhere, I suppose that Abney Park Cemetery claims the distinction. The tombstones are crowded together as closely as it seems possible, and yet they are constantly being added to, although the greater part of this cemetery is already over-full.

The first dissenting meeting-houses were in the City and its immediate neighbourhood. They were frequently but 'upper rooms' in narrow courts, and had no graveyards attached to them. But when the persecution of the Dissenters, under the *Act of Uniformity*, was relaxed, meeting-houses and chapels sprang up in every part of London, and these, in some cases, had burial-grounds adjoining them. A few of the larger grounds, such as Sheen's in Commercial Road, and the one in Globe Fields, were bought by private individuals and carried on as private speculations entirely apart from the chapels. But of the genuine Dissenters' graveyards, i e the little grounds attached to chapels and meeting-houses in London, there must have been at one time or another about eighty – there may have been more. This number of course represents but a very small portion of the meeting-houses themselves, which were in existence at the beginning of this century.

The only body of Nonconformists that has kept a careful account of its graveyards is the Society of Friends. They also treated their grounds and the remains in them with greater respect – except in one notable case to which I shall refer – and they kept them neat and clean, and do so still. A statement respecting their graveyards was made by representatives of the Society to the committee which sat in 1743, showing that they had considerable room in these grounds, and that they were careful not to allow less than 7 feet or 8 feet of earth above each coffin. The Friends attend to all matters connected with their meeting-houses and burial-grounds at their six weeks' meetings, and each of these grounds has been a Quakers' graveyard from the beginning, not changing hands, first belonging to one community and then another, as has been the case with so many of the chapel graveyards. The members of the Society have also exercised a most praiseworthy self-control by not wearing mourning, by avoiding useless expense at funerals, and ostentatious tombstones, memorials or epitaphs. Until about fifty years ago no tombstones were used at all, as at Long Lane, S.E.; then they used small flat ones, as at Hammersmith and Peckham; and finally they adopted small upright ones, all of the same shape, about a quarter of the size of the ordinary headstones in cemeteries. These may be seen at Ratcliff and Stoke Newington, the graveyard at the latter place, which still surrounds the Park Street meeting-house, being still in use.

Four of the Quakers' graveyards have entirely disappeared. The burial-ground for the Friends of Westminster was in Long Acre, by Castle Street. It passed out of their hands in 1757, and was built on. In rebuilding houses on the same spot, about four years ago, many human remains were disturbed. These were claimed by the Society, which was allowed to collect them and bury them at Isleworth. There was a little meeting-house with a graveyard attached in Wapping Street, which seems to have been used until about 1779, but was then demolished, the worshippers moving to the meeting in Brook Street, Ratcliff.

The other two burial-grounds which the Friends lost were in Worcester Street and Ewer Street, Southwark. The latter, although it adjoined their Old Park Meeting – which the King took as a guard house – may never have been used by them. At any rate, in 1839 it was in private hands, and eventually disappeared under the railway. The former, which dates from 1666, was very full, so that in 1733 the surface was raised above the original level. This was demolished when Southwark Street was made in 1860; and the London Bridge and Charing Cross Railway also runs over its site. The Friends then moved the remains and a number of coffins to their ground in Long Lane, Bermondsey. A most interesting report upon this removal was made by the Surveyor to the Quakers' six week meeting, in which are contained some excellent remarks upon the futility of burying in lead coffins, nine of these being found in the ground (see Appendix D). The graveyard had been disused since 1799.

The Quakers of the Bull and Mouth and Peel Divisions used a large ground near Bunhill fields, between Checquer Alley and Coleman – now Roscoe – Street. It was acquired in 1661 and many times added to, and was used extensively by them at the time of the Great Plague, when they had their own special dead-cart. George Fox's body was carried here in 1690, an orderly procession, numbering 4,000 persons, following to the grave. In 1840 a school was built in it, and the rest of the tale it grieves me to tell. A part of the burial-ground exists now, not half an acre in area. It is neatly laid out as a sort of private garden. Five thousand bodies were dug up in the other part and buried, with carbolic acid, in a corner of the existing piece, and the site from which they were removed is now covered with a Board School, a coffee-palace, houses, and shops, including the Bunhill Fields Memorial Buildings, erected in 1881. Although 12,000 Quakers were buried in the Coleman Street ground, including Edward Burrough and others who died as martyrs in Newgate Gaol, George Fox's grave was the only one marked by a stone, a small tablet on the wall, with the simple inscription 'G.F.'. This attracted visits from country Friends in such numbers that a zealous member of the Society named Robert Howard, 'pronounced it Nehushtan' and caused it to be destroyed.

The remainder of the Friends' burial-grounds are intact. The one in Baker's Row, Whitechapel in 1687, is now a recreation ground, and the one in Long Lane, Bermondsey, which was bought in 1697 for £120, has lately been laid out for the use of the public. In addition to these are, in London itself, five little grounds adjoining meeting-houses, in High Street, Deptford, in Brook Street, Ratcliff, in High Street, Wandsworth by the Creek, and in Hanover Street, Peckham Rye. All these grounds are neatly kept; the one in Peckham, which dates from 1821, is beautiful and illustrates what can be done with a disused and closed graveyard, not even visible from the road, when it is treated with proper care and respect. Many of the burial-grounds just outside London have been sold with the meeting-houses.

There are not many Roman Catholic burial-grounds in London apart from those attached to conventual establishments. St Mary's Church, Moorfields, has a very small churchyard and had two grounds, one in Bethnal Green, which has disappeared, and one in Wades Place, Poplar, now used as a school playground. This is the case also with a Roman Catholic burial-ground in Duncan Terrace, Islington, which has been asphalted for the use of the boys' school, some tombstones and a figure of the Virgin Mary being in an enclosure on the north side. There is a very large ground dedicated to All Souls,

A Prospect of the CHAPPLE in Tottenham Court Road Built A.D.1756 by Voluntary Subscriptions Rev.d M.r GEORGE WHITEFIELD Chaplain to the R.t Hon.ble the Countess of Huntingdon.

Whitfield's Tabernacle

by St Mary's Church, Cadogan Terrace, Chelsea, and a small one by the church in Parker's Row, Dockhead, S.E., Bermondsey, the garden here, which is now a recreation ground for the schools or the sisters, having also been used for burials. There is one in Woolwich, lately encroached upon through the enlargement of the school, where three lonely-looking graves are in a railed-in enclosure in the middle of a tar-paved yard; and there is also the ground behind St Thomas', Fulham, which is still in use.

But the burial-grounds adjoining Baptist, Wesleyan, Independent and other chapels, what shall be said of them? They have suffered terribly in the slaughter, and although many still exist, a very large number have entirely disappeared. Only three are open as public gardens – the Wesleyan ground in Cale Street, Whitechapel, St George's in the East, which was added to St George's churchyard garden in 1875; the ground behind the Independent Chapel by St Thomas' Square, Hackney; and the burial-ground adjoining Whitfield's Tabernacle, Tottenham Court Road, which was opened in February 1895 by the London County Council. One other graveyard was laid out as a garden, that adjoining Trinity Chapel, East India Dock Road, Canning Town, but it is now closed, no one at present undertaking its maintenance.

For the rest of the grounds, not only Methodist but also Congregationalist and above all Baptist, we must employ the 'diligent search in dirty corners', but all the searching in the world will not restore those that are gone – sold and built on. The Congregational Chapel on Stockwell Green, where all kinds of dirty rubbish, paper, iron building materials, the broken top of a lamp-post, etc., were lying about among the sinking graves; and a little ground in Church Street, Deptford, behind a chapel which belongs to a General Baptist (Unitarian) connection, whose creed I do not pretend to understand, but whose railings were so broken that a far larger visitor than I could have followed me through the gaps to behold broken tombstones, collections of unsavoury rubbish, and another specimen of the worn-out top of a lamp-post.

There were many other very untidy grounds, such as those by the Wesleyan Chapel in Liverpool Road, King's Cross, and the Congregational Chapel in Esher Street, Lambeth; but I think the three I have mentioned above would have been – in the Spring of 1895, at any rate – awarded the first, second, and third prizes in a competition for neglect; and in January 1896, I find these grounds are in much the same condition as they were then.

There is a large burial-ground behind a chapel in Cannon Street Road, E. The building passed into the hands of the Rector of St George's in the East, but was afterwards pulled down, and one of Raine's Foundation Schools was subsequently erected on its site. The burial-ground, in which so many Lascars (seamen from the East Indies) were interred, is now in three parts. One is a small playground for the school, the largest part is Messrs. Seaward Brothers' yard for their carts, and the third piece is a cooper's yard belonging to Messrs. Hasted and Sons. A similar kind of chapel in Penrose Street, Walworth, known for some time as St John's Episcopal Chapel, is now the studio of a scenic artist, while the large burial-ground in the rear is the depôt of the Newington Vestry, and is full of carts, manure, gravel, dust, stone, etc.

The East London Railway has swallowed up the

graveyards by Rose Lane Chapel, Stepney, and the Sabbatarian or Seventh Day Baptists' Chapel in Mill Yard by Leman Street, Whitechapel; the Medical School of Guy's Hospital, Southwark, is on the Mazepond Baptist Chapel ground; the site of one which adjoined the London Road Chapel, S.E., is now occupied by a tailor's shop, the next house being on the space where the chapel stood, and these two shops are easily picked out in a row as they are higher and newer than their neighbours on either side. A little Baptist graveyard in Dipping Alley, Horselydown, which had a baptistry in it, disappeared very many years ago; the site of the Baptist Chapel and burial ground in Worship Street, Shoreditch, forms part of the London and North Western Railway; a similar one in Broad Street, Wapping, is now, I believe, a milkman's yard, and was, for many years previously, the parish stoneyard; while the very crowded ground which used to be behind Buckingham Chapel, Palace Street, Westminster, has a brewery on it. There is a little graveyard in front of Maberley Chapel, Balls' Pond – now called Earlham Hall – but the three tombstones that are left in it are not only put upon the north wall of the chapel but have actually been painted with the wall.

I have mentioned that a few of the chapels have been replaced by schools, but I ought to mention that the graveyards behind Abney Chapel, Stoke Newington, N., Denmark Row Chapel, Coldharbour Lane, S.E., and the chapel in Hanbury Street, Mile End New Town, E., were closed for only a very few years before school buildings were erected on them. A small yard remains of the last named, but practically nothing is left of the others. The site of the graveyard in the rear of the chapel in Gloucester Street, Shoreditch has, together with that of the chapel itself, been merged into the premises of the Gas Light and Coke Company.

CHAPTER 7

BURIAL PLACES OF FOREIGNERS IN LONDON

It is only natural that in London, to which so many people from other countries have fled, and where so many have lived, worked and died, there should be evidences left of their places of interment. Solitary cases of their burial among Englishmen are, of course, to be met everywhere, and there are many such in the London graveyards. In Rotherhythe Churchyard is a well-known tombstone to the memory of Prince Lee-boo of the Pelew Islands, who died in 1784; in St Anne's, Soho, there is a tablet to Theodore, the last King of Corsica (*see* Appendix D); there is the grave of an Indian chief in the burial ground of St John's, Westminster, in Horseferry Road; and it is said that the first person interred in a part of Bishopsgate Churchyard was a Frenchman named Martin de la Tour, while this ground also used to contain a very old altar-tomb with a Persian inscription round it to the memory of Coya Shawware, a Persian merchant, who died in 1626. It is evident that for some time after his burial his son and other friends used to gather at the grave twice a day for prayer and funeral devotions, until driven away by the ridicule of the populace.

But there have been in London many special burial-grounds belonging to special groups of foreigners, and several of them remain. Foremost among these are the Jewish cemeteries. Until the year 1717, the time of

Henry II, the Jews in England were allowed only one burial-place. It was known as the Jews' Garden and was outside the Wall of London by Cripplegate, several acres being devoted to the purpose – a neighbourhood subsequently known by the name of Leyrestowe. When other places were permitted, this ground was built on, but the remembrance of it still lives on in the name of one street in the district, Jewin Street, reminding us of the time of the bitter persecutions which the Jews suffered and which are chronicled, to our shame, in English history. In the first place it is to be noticed that the Jews, as a race, are particularly pledged to preserve their burial places, a binding obligation handed down from the most ancient times, and any disturbance of the burial-grounds which now exist is not permitted. No doubt it was beyond their power to prevent the Jews' Garden from being covered with streets, its very size and position rendered it practically impossible to preserve, and it was probably annihilated during one of those periods when the Jews were expelled from England.

They also strictly observed the sanitary laws respecting burial laid down for them, and their cemeteries have not been over-crowded. Burial is only allowed at 6 feet from the surface of the ground, and only one body is allowed in each grave, one coffin not being placed above another, and this rule has been carried out in the Jewish burial-grounds in London – again with one exception. In the very large, very old graveyard in Brady Street, Bethnal Green – formerly called North Street – there are walls running through it, and the southern half is higher than the northern half, having quite a hilly appearance. The following is the explanation. This half was originally allotted to 'strangers', Jews who belonged to no special congregation. About thirty years after it was full, a layer of earth, 4 feet in depth, was added to the ground, and it was used all over again. As the coffins were placed 6 feet from the surface, there still remained 4 feet of earth between them and the old ones beneath. As a result of this curious and interesting arrangement, there may be seen, in several cases, two grave-stones standing back to back, which represent the two graves below them.

Within the Metropolitan area there are at present nine Jewish graveyards; there are others more lately acquired, and all are still in use, at Willesden, West Ham, Edmonton, Plashet and Golders Green, Hendon. The disused grounds which belong to the United Synagogue are those in Brady Street, Bethnal Green, Hoxton Street, N., Alderney Road, Mile End, E., and Grove Street, Hackney, E., and I cannot, unfortunately, call them well-kept, but the neatest is the one in Alderney Road. The one in Hoxton is very small. It was originally formed for the use of the Hamborough Synagogue, Fenchurch Street, and was first used about the year 1700. All these grounds are old; part of the one in Alderney Road dates from about 1700, while the Brady Street Cemetery was formed in 1795.

In Ball's Pond, Islington, is a small cemetery of the West London Congregation of British Jews, which is still in use. Here some very large and extravagant tombstones may be seen, and the ground is very neatly kept. In Fulham Road – Queen's Elm – is a dreary little ground belonging to the synagogue in St Alban's Place, S.W. I believe an occasional interment takes place here in reserved plots, but the congregation has provided itself with another cemetery at Edmonton. Some years back, before the *Disused Burial Grounds Act*, was in force, a row of shops was built on the west frontage of the ground, the only corpse lying in that part being removed to another place. No doubt the freehold worth of the land was considerable at that time, and therefore the congregation disregarded their scruples concerning this one deceased member.

In Bancroft Road, Mile End, is another dreary place which, although in so crowded a district, is still in use. When I last visited it I was told there was room for about four more graves! It belongs to the Maiden Lane Synagogue; none of these grounds except that at Ball's Pond, have proper paths in them; they have been entirely filled with graves, between which a few narrow lines like

Jewish Cemetery, Mile End

sheep-tracks wind about the grass.

Lastly there are the cemeteries of the Spanish and Portuguese Jews – one, closed for burials, behind Beth Holim Hospital in Mile End Road, and one, nearly five acres in extent and still in use, just beyond the People's Palace. These are neatly kept, the former, or at any rate, a part of it, being actually turned into a sort of garden for the patients in the hospital, with trees in it, paths and seats. The latter is bare of trees or shrubs but is divided into plots, with paths between them. Hitherto it has not been possible to secure any of the Jewish graveyards as public gardens, the feeling of the community is against it, but the day may yet come when the Council of the United Synagogue will allow the experiment to be tried.

The burial ground of Greeks in London is an enclosure in Norwood Cemetery, where some elaborate monuments may be seen. The Mohammedans can practise their rites at Woking. There is no special place at the present time, I believe, where Danes and Swedes are buried, but their churches, with surrounding churchyards,

Jewish Burial-ground behind the Beth Holim Hospital, Mile End

were situated close together, in Wellclose and Prince's Square, Whitechapel. The church in Prince's Square is still the Swedish Church of London (Eleanora) and there is a notice at the corner of a turning on the south side of Cable Street, St George's in the East, Whitechapel – 'Till Svenka Kyrkan.' But the building in Wellclose Square is no longer the Danish or Mariner's Church; the site is occupied by schools and mission houses in connection with St Paul's, Dock Street, the present seaman's church. Nor are there any tombstones in the garden, although it is certain that many Danes and many sailors were buried under the church and in a surrounding graveyard, which was probably an inner enclosure like that in Prince's Square.

The Flemish burial-ground was in the district of St Olave's, Southwark. It adjoined a chapel in Carter Lane, and, before its demolition, was used as an additional graveyard by the parishes of St Olave and St John, especially the former. When the railway to Greenwich was made, this ground disappeared, and part of its site

A South View of QUEEN ELIZABETH'S FREE GRAMMAR SCHOOL, in Tooley Street in the Parish of St Geo. Southwark; with a Plan of the adjacent Neighbourhood.

The Flemish Burial-ground, Carter Lane, about 1817

forms the approach to London Bridge Station.

In Milman's Row, Chelsea, there is a quaint and curious burial-ground belonging to the Moravians. The adjoining buildings have passed out of their hands, their present chapel being in Fetter Lane, E.C. In 1750 Count Zinzendorf purchased two acres of land – a part of the garden and stables of Beafort House – of Sir Hans Sloane, about one acre of which was set aside for burials and divided into four parts; the first for male infants and single brothers, the second for female infants and single sisters, the third for married brothers and widowers, and the fourth for married sisters and widows. The stones are flat on the grass and very small, not more than about 12 or 15 inches by 10 or 12 inches in size, and the ground has been closed for interments since about the year 1888.

There is no purely Dutch place of interment in London now. Besides the Dutch Church in Austin Friars – the survival of the priory of the Augustine Friars – which has lost its churchyard, they used to have a few chapels which seemed to change hands, sometimes belonging to Dutch and at other times to German congregations. Such was Zoar chapel in Great Alie Street, Whitechapel, which is now a Baptist conventicle. It had a fair-sized burial-ground behind it at the beginning of the century, the site of which is covered by houses and a forge. One day recently I knocked at the door of this chapel, hoping to be allowed to look round it in order to make sure that no part of the yard was left. The woman who opened it, when I politely asked if I might go in, said "No!" and slammed the door again at once. One meets with varied receptions in different places.

Two German churches, with graveyards attached, were also in this neighbourhood – the Lutheran 'St George's' in Little Alie Street, and the Protestant Reformed Church in Hooper Square. The latter has entirely disappeared, the railway covering its site. The former church still exists, with the little yard behind it, separated by a wall from the adjoining schoolyard, but the entrance from Little Alie Street has been bricked up.

The precinct of the Savoy (the Strand) had a distinctly foreign flavour about it, but the Savoy Chapel itself is now the only remnant left of the large group of buildings which were used at different time as palace, hospital, barracks, and prison, and finally demolished in 1877. The churchyard is probably even older than the church. It is now a neat little garden, in the possession of Her Majesty the Queen, as Duchess of Lancaster, and laid out, chiefly at her cost, for the use of the public. But the Savoy used to contain one, if not two, German chapels, besides a French Jesuit chapel and a meeting-place for Persian worship. The German church had a burial-ground on its west side, which was marked on the ordnance maps, except for the very latest, as it survived until 1876, when the human remains were removed to a cemetery at Colney Hatch. Now its site is covered by part of the new buildings which include the Savoy Chambers and the Medical Examination Hall.

We now turn to the French in London, and these have to be divided into the Roman Catholic and the

Huguenots. No doubt Frenchmen and French-women have been laid to rest in the burial-grounds attached to all the Roman Catholic churches, and especially in All Souls Cemetery, behind the chapel of St Mary, in Cadogan Place, Chelsea, which chapel was built by M. Voyaux de Franous, a French emigre clergyman, and consecrated in 1811. Large numbers were also interred at St Pancras, the eastern end of the old churchyard receiving, in consequence, the name of 'Catholic Pancras.' But this is the part which has been so much disturbed and appropriated by the Midland Railway company, and what remains of it is some dreary, dark slips under the railway arches, and groups and hillocks of tombstones which were moved into the western part of the ground.

About the year 1687 between thirteen and fourteen thousand French Protestants, driven from home by the intolerance of Louis XIV, settled in London, some in Spitalfields, others in the district of St Giles' and Seven Dials, in Stepney, and also in Wandsworth. There was a French church at Wandsworth, which fell into the hands of the Wesleyans, and the Huguenots who settled in this locality were chiefly engaged in trade as hatters. As a result we find their graves in Bethnal Green Churchyard and in other places, but especially in the East Hill burial-ground at Wandsworth.

Foreigners now have to be buried in the cemeteries, and many a strange service or ceremony has been held at the graveside of those who belong to other climes. The Jews and the Greeks are, I believe, the only community of strangers who still keep up separate burial-grounds of their own in London.

CHAPTER 8

HOSPITAL, ALMSHOUSE AND WORKHOUSE GROUNDS

When the Greyfriars, or Christ's Hospital, was set aside for 'poor children', and Bridewell for 'the correction of vagabonds', St Bartholomew's Hospital in the City and St Thomas' in Southwark were devoted to the care of 'the wounded, maimed, sick, and diseased'; and in these four benevolent institutions, which we owe so much to the short-lived but truly pious King Edward VI, there was provision made for the burial of the dead. It must be remembered that the quadrangle of Christ's Hospital, which is still surrounded by cloisters, was the burial-ground of the Greyfriars, but apart from this, for the boys of the school or the officers or servants, there was a small plot of ground set aside as a graveyard at the north-west corner of the block of buildings. This was demolished when the great hall was built in 1825 and if any of its site remains it is only a limited piece of the courtyard on the north side of the hall and the doctor's garden. A few tombstones are preserved in the passage leading to the doctor's house. At this time was formed the additional burial-ground at the western end of the churchyard of St Botolph, Aldersgate Street. But the churchyard adjoining Christ Church, and even the cloisters themselves, were used from time to time by the Hospital.

I think it probable that when St Bartholomew's Hospital was far smaller than it is now, burials took place in the cloisters, or rather in the large space in the middle of which the western wing was built. In a very interesting old plan of the precincts dated 1617, there is not only shown the 'Churchyarde for ye poore' in two pieces, about where the west wing is now, but also a large ground which is named Christ Churchyard to the south of this, but north of the City Wall. The hospital later on used the Bethlem burial-ground, and the ground set aside eventually as the hospital graveyard for the interment of unclaimed corpses is in Seward Street, Goswell Road. This was first used about 1740, and after being closed for burials, it was let as a carter's yard and was full of sheds and vans. Through the kindness of the Governors, it fell into the hands of the Metropolitan Public Gardens Association and it is now a children's recreation ground maintained by St Luke's Vestry.

The burial-ground of St Thomas' Hospital is at the corner of Mazepond; on part of it, St Olave's Rectory and Messrs. Bevington's leather warehouse were built; the remainder is leased to Guy's Hospital, and contains the treasurer's stables and an asphalted tennis-court for the use of the students.

Guy's Hospital burial-ground is in Snow's Fields, Bermondsey, and is now a large builder's yard, but there is a reasonable hope of its being secured before long as a recreation ground. The 'unclaimed corpses' found their last resting place very near home. In 1849 the whole of the southern part of the enclosure, quite an acre and a half, was the burial ground, and here, although it was closed by *Order of Council* in 1854, it appears that burials took place until about 1860, one of the present porters remembering his father acting as gravedigger. The medical school, the chaplain's house, and the nurses' home have all been built upon it, and it is sincerely hoped that no further encroachment will be permitted. The remaining part is the nurses' and students' garden and tennis-court, where they are in the habit of capering about in their short

Bethlehem Hospital 1896 – Demolished, now Liverpool
Street Station

times off duty, and where it sometimes happens that the
grass gives way beneath them – an ordinary occurrence
when the sub-soil is inhabited by coffins!

Bridewell also had its burial-ground, where the lazy
and evil were interred. It is at the corner of Dorset and
Tudor Streets, near the Thames Embankment, and it is
an untidy yard, boarded off from the street with a high
advertisement hoarding, and in the occupation of a
builder.

The Bethlem burial-ground had a more interesting
history. In 1569 Sir Thomas Roe, Merchant Tailor and
Mayor, gave about one acre of land in the Moorfields 'for
the Burial Ease to such parishes in London as wanted
convenient ground.' It was especially intended for the
parish of St Botolph's, Bishopgate, and was probably used
for the interment of lunatics from the neighbouring asylum,
besides being used by St Bartholomew's Hospital. But the
Churchyard and the Asylum have disappeared, Liverpool
Street Station having taken their place, and hundreds of

the Great Eastern Railway goods vans daily roll over the mouldering remains of the departed citizens.

Very different to the fate of these hospital burial-grounds is that of another I will mention. Facing Queen's Road, Chelsea, is the long, narrow graveyard of the Chelsea Hospital. It is neatly kept, with good grass and trees. Here many a venerable pensioner has been laid to rest, and although it can no longer be used for burials, it serves to remind the living of their brethren who have gone before them. There are some fine monuments and epitaphs to very long-lived invalids, two aged 112, one 111, one 107, and so on. One pensioner, who died in 1732, named William Hiseman, and aged 112, was 'a veteran, if ever soldier was.' It is recorded that he took himself a wife when he was above 100 years old!

On the south side of the Thames there are some other burial-grounds which should be mentioned here. Greenwich Hospital possesses no fewer than three cemeteries. In 1707 Prince George of Denmark gave a plot of ground for the purpose, measuring 660 by 132 feet. This is on the west side of the Royal Naval School. It is enclosed and full of tombstones. But in 1747 an extra two and a half acres, surrounding the old ground, were appropriated for interments. The gate from the school playground is generally open.

Then there is the Hospital Cemetery in West Combe, nearly six acres in size, and first used in 1857. The burial-ground of God's Gift College, Dulwich, is at the corner of Court Lane. It dates from about 1700 and is a picturesque, well-kept little ground, with several handsome altar tombs in it. The cemetery of Morden College, Blackheath, founded for decayed merchants about 1695, also exists. It is about a quarter of an acre in size, with about eighty tombstones, but the graves have been levelled and the ground, though still walled round, forms part of the College gardens.

There were several almhouse graveyards in London, including the 'College yard' for St Saviour's Almhouses in Southwark, which is now a builder's store-yard in Park

Street, and over which the London, Brighton, and South Coast Railway passes on arches, and one behind the Goldsmith's Almhouses, now covered by the workmen's dwellings on the west side of Goldsmith Row, Shoreditch. The frightfully crowded 'almshouse ground' in Clement's Lane formed part of the site of the new Law Courts, while one in Crown Street, Soho, adjoining St Martin's Almshouses, disappeared when the French Chapel was built, and has now been lost in Charing Cross Road. In order to enter the almshouses in White Horse Street, Stepney, it is necessary to pass through a graveyard, and it cannot be a lively outlook for the pensioners, who have gravestones just under their windows. It was connected with the Independent Chapel and first used in 1781.

Perhaps the most interesting of these burial-grounds is one belonging to the Bancroft Almshouses in Mile End Road. The fate of the asylum itself is well known; it has been replaced by the People's Palace, and the improvement from an antiquarian or architectural point of view is nil. The recent interest taken in the proposed destruction of the Trinity Hospital in Mile End Road points to the fact that the pendulum of public opinion is now swinging towards the preservation of historical buildings. The graveyard of Bancroft's Almshouses was a long strip on the eastern side. Part of it has been merged into the roadway. St Benet's Church, consecrated in 1872, the Hall and Vicarage were built upon it, and the bones of the pensioners are under the Vicarage garden. The northernmost point of the graveyard is enclosed and roofed over, and forms a little yard where flagstaffs, etc., are stored. But between this and the wall of the Vicarage there is a piece open to the road, with some heaps of stone in it and rubbish. There are, at any rate, four gravestones left against the wall, and there may be others behind the stones; but I daresay it is only a very small proportion of those who pass in and out of the Palace who have ever noticed this relic of the Bancroft Almshouses.

In a large number of the London parishes it is necessary to have 'poor grounds', i.e. graveyards where bodies could be interred at a trifling cost or entirely at the cost of the parish; for, notwithstanding the great dislike of the poor to a 'pauper's funeral', and the efforts they will make to avoid it, there always have been cases in which no other sort of funeral can be arranged. Some of the 'poor grounds' were attached to the workhouses, others were merely a part of the parish churchyards, while others again were older additional burial-grounds secured by the parishes before the days of workhouses.

The workhouse of St Andrew's, Holborn, was in Shoe Lane, and its adjoining graveyard gave way to the Farringdon Market, which, in its turn, has been supplanted by a new street called Farringdon Avenue. The workhouse ground of St Sepulchre's, Holborn, together with another additional graveyard belonging to the parish, was in Durham Yard, and the sites of both of them have disappeared in the goods depot of the Great Northern Railway.

The burial-grounds by the workhouses of Shoreditch, St Paul's, Covent Garden, and St Giles', in Short's Gardens, have also disappeared; so also has the one allotted to the use of St James' Workhouse in Poland Street, which was a part of the old pest-field, although a remnant of the pest-field exists still as the workhouse garden. The original Whitechapel Workhouse was built in 1768 on a burial-ground, and then a plot of land immediately to the north was set aside for a poor ground, and consecrated in 1796. This in turn became the playground of the Davenant Schools, one of which, facing St Mary's Street, was built in it. A recent addition to the other school has also encroached on the burial ground. In 1832 cholera cases were interred in an adjoining piece of ground, which was probably what is now used as a stoneyard, and is full of carts.

The workhouse graveyard belonging to St Clement Danes, was in Portugal Street. The workhouse itself was re-adapted and re-opened as King's College Hospital, but the burial-ground was used until its condition was so loathsome, and the burning of coffins and

Headquarters of the Metropolitan Fire Brigade

mutilation of bodies was of such every-day occurrence, that it must have been one of the very worst places in London. It is now the garden or courtyard and approach, between the hospital and Portugal Street.

The burial-ground attached to the Workhouse of St Saviour's, Southwark – which may have been the old Baptist burial-ground in Bandy Leg Walk, which existed in 1729 – has a curious history. The workhouse was supplanted by Winchester House, the palace of the bishops when South London was in their diocese, the old Winchester House, nearer the river, having been destroyed. This in time became a hat manufactory, the burial-ground remaining as a garden situated between the building and Southwark Bridge Road. Finally the site was secured by the Metropolitan Board of Works for the Central Fire Brigade Station (see Appendix D), and what is now left of the burial ground is the garden or courtyard between the new buildings which face the road and the old house behind them. If the paupers and the bishops and the factory hands did not succeed in frightening away the ghosts of the departed, they must have a sorry time of it now, when the call-bells from all parts of London bring out the engines and the men who fight the flames!

Of the parochial 'poor houses' not adjoining workhouses, a few are worth noticing. St Saviour's, Southwark, in addition to the workhouse ground, the College or Almshouse ground, and the churchyard itself, which was, from time to time added to, curtailed and used for markets, possessed still another graveyard, the famous Crossed Bones ground in Union Street, referred to by John Stow as having been made 'far from the Parish Church' for the interment of the low women who frequented the neighbourhood. It subsequently became the parish poor-ground, and after having been in use, and very much over-crowded, for upwards of 200 years, it was closed by *Order in Council* dated October 24, 1853. In a report upon the state of this ground the previous year, it is stated that 'it is crowded with dead, and many fragments of undecayed bones, some even entire, are mixed up with the earth of the mounds over the graves, and it can be considered only as a convenient place for getting rid of the dead, but it bears no marks of ever having been set apart as a place of Christian sepulchre.' The Cross Bones ground passed out of the hands of the rector several years ago and was sold as a building site, but building operations were opposed and stopped. Schools were erected in it before it was closed for burials. It has been made the subject of much litigation, and it now stands vacant, waiting for someone to purchase it as a playground, and used in the meantime as the site for fairs, merry-go-rounds and cheap shows.

The 'poor ground' for the parish of St George the Martyr, Southwark, is a square plot of land, now a little public garden in Tabard Street. It was originally the burial-ground of the adjoining Lock Hospital before that building was removed in 1809 to Knightsbridge, whence, later on, it was again moved to Harrow Road. It has been said by some that the little cemetery was even older than the hospital, and may have been used for interments during no fewer than eight centuries.

The Cripplegate 'poor ground' or the 'upper churchyard of St Giles' was in Bear and Ragged Staff Yard – afterwards called Warwick Place – out of Whitecross Street, and was first used in 1636. It was very much over-crowded, so much so that it was more than once shut up for a few years as full, but always re-opened again. A part of the site is now occupied by the northern half of the church of St Mary, Charterhouse, and by its mission-house, there being only a tar-paved pathway round these buildings to represent the rest of the ground. The church was built in 1864; there are human remains within six inches of the surface of the ground, several having been dug up and put in a vault which is under the mission house, and the entrance to which is closed with a very large flat stone bearing the date 1865. The mission-house is giving way already, and it has large cracks in it, for a vault of this kind is not a good foundation.

The parish of St James', Clerkenwell, had a very small 'poor ground' in Ray Street, which was bought in 1755 for £340, and was consecrated eight years later. It was 800 square yards in area and was approached through a private house occupied by a butcher 'who had his slaughter-house and stable at the back, and immediately adjoining the burial-ground.' In about the year 1824 it was found that several bodies had been exhumed and placed in the stable; this caused a scandal in the neighbourhood, and the man and his business were ruined. When Farringdon Street and the Metropolitan Railway were made, the site of the ground in Ray Street, together with Ray Street itself, entirely disappeared, and the 'sleepers of the railway' are laid over the 'sleepers in death.' The burial-ground had already been done away with, the Clerkenwell Commissioners having taken it for public improvement, when they collected the remains into one spot and erected a plain mausoleum over them.

In early days it seems to have been the custom for patients entering the large hospitals to pay a sum of

money down for possible funeral expenses, except in
the case of sudden accident. Later on a security given
by a householder was considered sufficient, but now no
such arrangement is needed. The sum demanded at St
Bartholomew's was 17s.6d and at Guy's £1 was paid.
At Westminster Hospital and at the Lock (Hyde Park
Corner), from which some patients may have been buried
in what is now called Knightsbridge Green, no security
was asked, but at the Bethlem Hospital, an entrance of
£100 had to be paid for board, funeral expenses, etc. In
case of death at a London hospital at the present time,
the friends or relatives are expected to remove and bury
the body and this has often led to a good deal of difficulty,
one body being claimed by various people, because the
the person who buries it can often secure the insurance
money. Bodies which are now unclaimed – and at St
Bartholomew's there are about eight a year – are buried
in a cemetery at the cost of the hospital.

CHAPTER 9

PRIVATE CEMETERIES

There are two chief senses in which the word 'private' may be taken. It denotes what belongs to a particular person, family, or institution apart from the general public – thus we say a 'private chapel', a 'private drive', and so on. It also means that which has been set into being by a private person, and which is, therefore, a private speculation. Into these two classes I can divide the graveyards which are to be dealt with in the chapter.

The Romans preserved the right of erecting tombs in their country residences. Their very stringent laws prevented them from burying the dead inside the cities, except certain classes of very privileged persons, but as long as the interment took place outside the walls, it seems, at one time, to have mattered little where a tomb was set up. This practice was put a stop to in the time of Duillius, and sepulchres were no longer allowed in fields and private grounds, as it was found that the custom was tending to diminish the area of land available for cultivation.

I think that such a practice was never general in London or the surrounding district, but there are a few cases in which something of the sort took place. In Wood's *Ecclesiastical Antiquities*, it is stated that there was a cemetery at Somerset House, Strand, for the Catholic members of Queen Henrietta Maria's household (1626). It is certain that the vaults under the palace chapel were used, as they were closed for interments in

1777 (fourteen burials having taken place in fifty-seven years), and if there was also a cemetery, the use of which was in this way restricted, it may fairly be called private. It is possible however that this may have been a part of the original churchyard of St Mary le Strand. The site has now disappeared, the present building of Somerset House being far more extended than was the old one.

Another curious private ground, also used by the Romanists, was the garden of Hundsdon House, the French Embassy, in Blackfriars. In 1623 the floor of a neighbouring Jesuit chapel gave way and about 23 persons were killed. Stow says that 20 bodies, of the poorer people, were buried on the spot. Malcolm states that 44 were buried in the courtyard before the Ambassador's house, and 15 in his garden. Brayley's version is that some were buried in a burying place 'within the Spanish Ambassador's house in Holborn,' and that two great pits were dug, one in the forecourt of the French Ambassador's house, 18 feet by 12 feet, where 44 were interred, the other in the garden behind, 12 feet by 8 feet. Wood gives the number of those buried in these pits as 47. It was, at any rate, a curious and summary way of disposing of the bodies of those who had so suddenly lost their lives.

I only know of one burial-ground in London which is so strictly private as to have only one grave in it. In Retreat Place, Hackney, a quiet corner near the Unitarian Church, there is a row of twelve almshouses, founded by Samuel Robinson in 1812 'for the widows of Dissenting ministers professing Calvinistic doctrines.' In front of this establishment is a neatly kept grassed plot, and in the centre is a large altar tomb – not erected for the use of the ministers' widows, but containing the mortal remains of Samuel Robinson himself, who died in 1833, and of his own widow who survived him for three years. For my own part I should prefer the enclosure without the grave, but perhaps the widows like to be daily reminded of their benefactor.

There are, no doubt, many private gardens and yards in London in which burials have taken place, surreptitiously if not openly. Only recently an undertaker was remanded for having been in the habit of temporarily depositing the bodies of stillborn infants in his own back premises until as such time as there should be enough to make it worth while for him to give them a decent burial. But numerous as these instances may be, it is difficult to get any record of them.

Convent burial-grounds are very private, as mentioned in an earlier chapter.

In Milbank Penitentiary a space, 432 square yards in extent, was set aside as a graveyard, in which there was ordinarily rather over one burial per month. This particular piece of ground is to be preserved when the new buildings are erected on the site of the prison; it will probably belong to the London School Board. Newgate Prison burial-ground is still in use. It is a passage in the prison, 10 feet wide and 85 feet long, in which are interred, with a plentiful supply of quicklime, the bodies of those who are executed within the walls (see Appendix D).

This reminds me of the gallows which stood for so many years at the Tyburn turnpike, the site of which is still marked by a stone in the Bayswater Road, a few yards west of the Marble Arch. Those who were executed here – there were 24 in 1729 – were buried on the spot, and this extraordinary burial-ground was situated at the point now occupied by the house at the corner of Edgware Road and Upper Bryanston Street (see Appendix D). On their way to the gallows the poor criminals received a present of a large bowl of ale, called St Giles' bowl, from the lazar hospital of St Giles, which was situated close to where the church now stands (the origin of the popular saying 'one for the road!').

By the close of the last century the London churchyards and the additional burial-grounds provided by the parishes were becoming over-crowded, and it was greatly owing to their existence and to their abuse, that the agitation arose which finally led to the passing of the Act to amend the Laws concerning the Burial of the Dead in the Metropolis, under which the metropolitan burial-grounds were closed. It then occurred to some adventurers to start cemeteries as private speculations, which was so successful that it was imitated in different parts of London, until by the year 1835 there must have been at least fourteen burial-grounds in London carried on by private persons, besides some additional chapels with vaults under them, conducted in the same way. A few of these grounds originated in connection with neighbouring places of worship, but were subsequently bought by private persons. In Central London there were (1) Spa Fields, Clerkenwell; (2) Thomas' burial-ground, Golden Lane; (3) New City Bunhill Fields, or the City of London burial-ground, Golden Lane.

In North London there was (4) the New or Little Bunhill Fields, Church Street, Islington. In East London there were (5) Sheen's burial-ground, Whitechapel; (6) Victoria Park Cemetery, Bethnal Green; (7) the East London Cemetery, or Beamont's ground, Mile End; (8) Globe Fields burial-ground, Mile End Old Town; (9) The North-east London Cemetery, or Cambridge Heath burial-ground, or Peel Grove burial-ground, or Keldy's Ground, Bethnal Green; (10) Gibraltar Walk burial-ground, Bethnal Green; (11) Ebenezer Chapel Ground, Ratcliff Highway. And in South London (12) Butler's burial-ground, Horselydown, or St John's; (13) the New Bunhill fields, or Hoole and Martin's ground, Deverell Street, New Kent Road; and (14) a ground in Ewer Street, Southwark.

The charges for interments in these places were generally slightly lower than in the churchyards, in order to attract customers, and those who officiated at the funerals were, in many cases, not ministers of religion at all. In Butler's burial-ground, for instance, the person who read the burial service (of the Church of England) wore a surplice, but he was merely an employee of the undertaker, who also acted as porter. In Hoole and Martin's ground a Mr Thomas Jenner was employed to officiate at funerals for £20 a year. He also read the burial service of the Church of England, but he was by trade a shoemaker, or a pattenmaker, whose shop was nearby.

Spa Fields Playround

The owners of these private grounds were naturally tempted to crowd them to excess, and it is impossible to think of what took place in some of them without shuddering. No doubt practices as vile, as unwholesome, and as irreverent were carried on in many of the churchyards; but the overcrowding of the private grounds is so associated with the idea of private gloating over private possessions over private gains that it is more repulsive.

One of the most notoriously offensive spots in London was Enon Chapel, Clement's Lane, near the Monument. The chapel was built, and the vaults beneath it were made, as a speculation by a dissenting minister named Howse. The burial fees were small, and the place was resorted to by the poor, as many as nine or ten burials often taking place on a Sunday afternoon. The space available for coffins was, at the highest computation, 59 feet by 29 feet, with a depth of 6 feet, and no fewer than 20,000 coffins were deposited there. In order to accomplish this herculean task it was the common practice to burn the older coffins in the minister's house, under his copper (a large, bowl-shaped container used for washing clothes, having a small fire grate beneath it), and in his fireplaces. Between the coffins and the floor of the chapel there was nothing but the boards. In time the effluvium (stench) in the chapel became intolerable, and no one attended the services, but the vaults were still used for interments, so that 'more money was made from the dead than from the living' – a state of affairs which existed in many of the private burial-places of the Metropolis.

As I shall have to refer again to the condition of these grounds, in speaking of the closing of graveyards in London, I will not enlarge upon it any further here, except to quote from the evidence brought before the Select Committee which sat in 1842 to consider the *Interment in Towns*, respecting the Globe Fields burial-ground in Mile End, which is merely one example out of sixty-five examinations.

William Miller was called in and examined by the Chairman and Members, as follows:

What is your occupation? – A jobbing labouring man, when I can get anything to do.
Have you been a grave-digger in Globe Fields, Mile End? – Yes.
Is that a private burial-ground? – Yes.
To whom does it belong? – Mr. Thomas Tagg.
Have many pits been dug in it for the depositing of bodies previously interred? – Yes.
Where did they come from? – Out of the coffins which were emptied for others to go into the graves.
Were the coffins chucked in with them? – No, they were broken up and burnt.
Were they bones, or bodies, that were interred? – Yes; the bones and bodies as well.
Were they entire, or in a state of decomposition? – Some were dry bones, and some were perfect.

What did you do with them? – Chucked them into the pit.

What sort of pit? – A deep, square pit about four feet wide and seven or eight feet deep.

How many bodies did you chuck in? – I cannot say, they were so numerous; each pit would hold about a dozen.

How many of these pits did you dig? – I suppose I dug a matter of 20 myself.

How near to the surface of the earth did these dead bodies or bones come?-

Within about two feet.

What is the size of this ground? – It is rather better than half an acre.

How many bodies are buried in that ground within a year? – I cannot say; I suppose there are 14,000 buried in that ground.

How long has it been open? – Since the year 1820.

Do you recollect any circumstance which occurred there about the month of October, 1839? – Yes.

Will you state it to the Committee? – Some boys were at work there; a policeman on the railroad happened to see them in the act of taking some bones out of baskets, and got a policeman in the police force of the metropolis, and sent him in and seized the boys with a bag of nails and plates off the coffins, going away to sell them, and going to sell the bones.

To what purpose are the bones applied? – I do not know.

What is done with the wood of the coffins? – Burnt for their own private use.

By whom? – By the sexton.

Is it burnt in the sexton's house? – Yes.

What was done with the iron or metal handles of the coffins? – They were burnt on the coffins when I was there, and were thrown out among the ashes about the ground anywhere.

Who performs the burial-service over the dead?
– A gentleman by the name of Cauch.
Does he reside there? – No, he resides opposite.
What is he? – I do not know that he is anything; he
has formerly been a shoemaker.
Does he put on a gown when he buries the dead?
– Yes, a surplice.
What service does he read? – The regular Church
service.
Were you in the habit of performing this grave-
digging without the use of spirits? – No; we were
obliged to be half groggy to do it, and we cheered
one another and sung to one another.
You found the work so disgusting you were obliged
to be half drunk? – Yes.

And so on. Many of the revelations made to this committee
were so revolting that they are best forgotten. It is, perhaps,
only fair to say that this particular man's evidence was
contradicted by Mr. Thomas Tagg, the owner of the
ground, but it was subsequently corroborated by other
and disinterested parties.

The fate of these fourteen grounds has been a varied
one. Thomas's has gone, and its site is occupied by a
large building, chiefly a shoe factory, in the north side
of Playhouse Yard, and immediately to the west of the
church known as St Mary's Charterhouse. Sheen's is now
the yard of Messrs. Fairclough, carters, off Commercial
Road, and there are some stables and sheds in it. It was,
some years back, a cooperage. Peel Grove is smaller than
it was, and what is left is a builder's yard about an acre
in extent, the remainder of the space having been built
on. The very small ground by Ebenezer Chapel, near St
George's in the East, is also a timber yard, the chapel
itself having long since fallen into disuse.

Over half of the Globe Fields ground, the Great Eastern
Railway runs; the remainder is a bare yard with several
miserable tombstones in it, and quantities of rubbish. It

is fast closed behind an iron gate of colossal proportions, and it daily becomes more neglected and untidy. Little Bunhill Fields in Islington is divided into several parts; one division belongs to the General Post Office, and contains parcel-vans, etc.; other parts are let or sold as builders' yards or are lying vacant. New Bunhill Fields, near New Kent Road, has been through many vicissitudes; it was very much over-crowded with bodies, and in the vaults under the chapel, burials used to take place 'on lease' i.e. £1 would be paid for a coffin to be deposited for six months, after which no enquiries were to be made. As soon as the ground was closed, it became a timber-yard, and the chapel in it was used as a saw-mill. Now the sawing goes on in an adjoining shed and the chapel belongs to the Salvation Army, the graveyard being still covered with high stacks of timber.

The City of London ground in Golden Lane, which was only used for about twenty years, is divided; the part situated in the parish of St Luke's belongs to Messrs. Sutton & Co., and is full of carts, the greater part of it being roofed in. The part situated within the City boundary forms the site of the City Mortuary and Coroner's Court, with a neatly kept yard between the two buildings. Gibraltar Walk burial-ground, Bethnal Green Road, has only had small slices cut off it and doled out as yards, etc., for the surrounding houses. The main portion is a neglected jungle, forming a sort of private garden to the big house which opens on to it, and in which the owner of the ground lives.

In order to see Butler's burial-ground it is necessary to go down Coxon's Place, Horselydown, where two yards will be found. One is a small builder's yard with 'Beware of the Dog' on the gate. Once I doubted the existence of the dog, and pushed open this gate, but he was there in full vigour, and I speedily fled. The adjoining yard, which is much bigger, is Messrs. Zurhoost's cooperage, and is full of barrels. There were vaults used for burials under the three or four of the houses. They can still be seen, and are now, apparently, dwelling-places for the living.

The graveyard in Ewer Street has disappeared under the London Bridge and Charing Cross Station.

The East London Cemetery in Shandy Street, Mile End, is a recreation ground chiefly for children. So is Spa Fields, Clerkenwell, which was one of the most crowded burial-grounds in London, after having been a fashionable tea-garden, and before being used as a volunteer drill-ground. Both these grounds were secured and laid out by the Metropolitan Public Gardens Association and are maintained by the London County Council.

Such is also the history of Victoria Park Cemetery, a space of 11½ acres, and by far the largest of the private burial-grounds. In this ground it was stated that, on every Sunday in the year 1856, 130 bodies were interred. After years of negotiation and much difficulty, the Metropolitan Public Gardens Association secured it and converted it from a dreary waste of crumbling tombstones and sinking graves into a charming little park for the people of Bethnal Green. It was opened by HRH the Duke of York in July 1894, and the County Council maintains it, having re-christened it Meath Gardens.

It needs hardly to be pointed out that in very few of the spaces I have just described, are any tombstones to be found. To a casual observer they are utterly unrecognisable as burial-grounds, and it is many years since such relics can have existed in them. When, for instance, a burial-ground becomes a builder's yard, tombstones are very much in the way and they are soon converted into paving stones. Some years ago a few inscriptions were still legible on the stones which paved the way to Spa Fields from Exmouth Street, but by this time even these must have worn away. But if it is denied by the owners of these yards that they are burial-grounds, there is one method of proving it which soon dispels all doubt, and that is by digging down into the soil. It will not be necessary to make any deep excavation before the spade turns up some earth mixed with human remains, which, once seen, are always recognisable.

CHAPTER 10

THE CLOSING OF BURIAL GROUNDS AND VAULTS

By the commencement of the present century the minds of thoughtful men on the Continent and in England began to be exercised about the over-crowded state of the graveyards in the towns, and their very unwholesome effect upon those who lived near them. We owe the agitation which finally led to the closing of the London graveyards mainly to the untiring zeal of a surgeon of Drury Lane, George Alfred Walker. His work lay among the poor of the district, and he was led to believe that the frequent occurrences of what he called typhus and similar maladies, was due in great measure to the large number of over-crowded burial-grounds which existed in the neighbourhood. He made a very careful study of the subject, he gathered information from France, Germany, and other countries, he visited a large number of the worst graveyards in London and made searching inquiries respecting them. Having become familiar with the practices that were carried on in these places, he brought out a book dealing with the whole question in the year 1839, the title-page of which fully explains its purpose. It is as follows:

GATHERINGS FROM GRAVEYARDS
Particularly those of London
With a concise history on the modes of Interment among different Nations from the earliest periods, and a detail of dangerous and fatal results

produced by the unwise and revolting custom
of inhuming the dead in the midst of the living.

The question was taken up from purely philanthropic
motives. Walker was not connected with, or interested
in, any particular cemetery, but he was 'fully convinced
of the necessity for legislative interference to destroy the
present dangerous system.'

Walker collected details of many cases of death and
illness directly attributable to contact with human remains
in a state of putrefaction. It was certain that gravediggers
held their lives in their hands. The more experienced of
them, when they 'bored' or 'tapped' i.e. made a hole in a
coffin, immediately fled to a distance and remained away
until they considered that the harmful exhalations would
have been sufficiently distributed into the air for them
to continue their unpleasant work in comparitive safety.
Another custom was to burn papers, etc., in graves and
vaults, while some men were in the habit of holding rue
or garlic in their mouths. But they generally suffered from
bad health, were frequently seriously ill, and sometimes
died from the direct effects of the poison they had inhaled.
They were also much addicted to drink, and very many
were accustomed to say that they could not do their work
without the help of spirits.

After making the following general statement, Walker
carefully described between forty and fifty of the most
crowded of the metropolitan burial-places, and especially
those in his own district; 'although willing to admit that the
neighbourhood of slaughter-houses – the decomposition
of vegetable substances – the narrowness of the streets,
and the filth and poverty of some of the inhabitants,
greatly contribute to the furtherance of the mischief
(typhus fever), I felt convinced that the grand cause of all
the evil was the immediate proximity of the burial-places,
public as well as private.'

It is quite unnecessary to repeat the descriptions,
they are much alike; I will only give one as a specimen,
which is free from obnoxious details.

The Churchyard of St. Ann, Soho, in 1810

'St Ann's, Soho: there is only one burying-ground belonging to this parish; it is walled in on the side next to Prince's Street; close to this wall is the bone-house; rotten coffin wood and fragments of bones are scattered about. Some graves are only partly filled up, and left in that state, intended, probably, for paupers. The ground is very full, and is considerably raised above its original level; it is overlooked by houses thickly inhabited. The inhabitants of the neighbourhood have frequently complained of the past and present condition of this place.'

Some of his descriptions were thought at the time to be exaggerated, but they were fully corroborated in the evidence given before the Parliamentary Committee which sat in 1842. Such a note as the following is instructive; 'Ground in immediate proximity to this place – Bermondsey Churchyard – is advertised to be let on lease for building purposes.' And yet some of the very burial-grounds themselves have since become the sites for streets and houses!

It would not be fair to give the reader the impression that Walker was the first to speak of the unwholesome condition of London's graveyards. Here is a quotation from a sermon preached by Bishop Latimer in 1552; 'The citizens of Naim had their burying-places within the city, which, no doubt, is a laudable thing; and I do marvel that London, being so great a city, hath not a burial-place without; for no doubt it is an unwholesome thing to bury within the city, especially at such time when there be great sicknesses, and many die together. I think verily that many a man taketh his death in St Paul's Churchyard, and this I speak of experience, for I myself, when I have been there on some mornings to hear the sermons, have felt such an ill-savoured, unwholesome savour, that I was the worse for it a great while after; and I think no less, but it is the occasion of great sickness and disease.' And from his time onwards allusions were made, in sermons and discourses, by ministers and physicians, to the danger of contact with decaying animal substances.

Walker stuck to his ground manfully. He gathered round him a few leading men of the day, who formed themselves into a Society for the Abolition of Burial in Towns, and he delivered a series of able lectures upon the subject and continued to make inquiries and to expose practices carried on in various grounds. Spa Fields, for instance, was taken as a specimen, and a pamphlet was issued showing how it was the custom to burn bodies out of sight behind a brick enclosure, and how the gravestones were moved about to give an appearance of emptiness in certain parts of the ground. It was computed that, by burning coffins, mutilating remains, and using vast quantities of quicklime, at least 80,000 corpses had been put into a space fitted to hold 1000.

In 1842 and 1843 a Royal Commission was sitting upon the question of the *Health of Towns and the Sanitary Condition of the Labouring Classes*, and a Select

Committee was appointed 'to consider the expediency of framing some Legislative Enactments, due respect being paid to the rights of the Clergy, to remedy the evils arising from the Interment of Bodies within the Precincts of large Towns or of Places densely populated.' One extract from the eventual report said 'After long and patient investigation, Your Committee cannot arrive at any other conclusion than that the nuisance of Interments in large Towns, and the injury arising from the practice, are fully proved. No time ought to be lost by the Legislature in applying a remedy.' And yet it was not until 1852 that the *Act to Amend the Laws concerning the Burial of the Dead in the Metropolis*, commonly known as the *Burials Act*, 15 and 16 Victoria, was passed.

Then the Home Secretary was besieged with memorials and letters from those who resided in various parts of London, praying for the Act to be put in force in the burial-grounds in their own neighbourhoods, besides applications for permission to open cemeteries on the outskirts of town. The same dreary and miserable stories of the over-crowding of graveyards and the indecent practices carried on in them were again brought to light, and it must not be supposed that the grounds in the west of London were any better than those in the centre, the east or the south. The description given by five medical men of the burial-ground belonging to St George's, Hanover Square, which is situated on the north side of Bayswater Road, together with the letters written about it, could hardly be exceeded. And yet this ground was, or rather is, in a fashionable neighbourhood, close to the Marble Arch, and surrounded by houses let at very high rentals. It is certain that it was a common custom to move freshly-buried corpses from the more expensive part of the ground to the cheaper part, used for paupers and others, thus making room for more graves for which the higher fees were paid.

On the 13 January 1853 Islington Churchyard was closed for burials, and from that time forward the notices were issued for the cessation of interments in vaults and graveyards all over London, and the list which was printed of all the burial-grounds in London still open for interments on January 1, 1855 was quite a short one. By that date eight of the large cemeteries had been opened and were in use.

When once closed for burials the question naturally arose as to what to do with the grounds. The following clause was inserted into one of the *Burial Acts*; 'In every case in which any order in Council has been or shall hereafter by issued for the discontinuance of burials in any churchyard or burial-ground, the Burial Board or Churchwardens, as the case may be, shall maintain such churchyard or burial-ground of any parish in decent order, and also do the necessary repairs of the walls and other fences thereof, and the costs and expenses shall be repaid by the Overseers upon the certificate of the Burial Board or Churchwardens, as the case may be, out of the rate made for the relief of the poor of the parish or place in which such churchyard or burial-ground is situate, unless there shall be some other fund legally chargeable with such costs and expenses.'

So the churchyards remained, useless, closed and dreary; no one went into them, the children gazed at them through the palings, and their parents deposited waste-paper, dead cats, rotten food, old clothes, etc. in them, and it was twenty years after they had been shut up before any of the disused graveyards were converted into public gardens.

The closing of the burial-grounds included the closing of the vaults. There is hardly a church in London, and but few chapels, with a graveyard attached, which had not also vaults used for interments under the building, and there are many churches and chapels which had vaults but not churchyards.

The earliest burials took place in the churchyards, the south side being always the favourite. It seems originally to have been customary to bury only stillborn infants, felons and suicides on the north side of the building. It became the fashion of later times to bury in or under the church, and the first place used was the porch. But when once the custom was established, the inside of the church became the privileged place, and the most honoured dead were laid nearest the altar. The ancient crypts, such as those at St Bartholomew's and Clerkenwell, were not, I imagine, originally intended for burying in, although coffins were put in them later on. But the vaults, such as those under the City churches and the parish churches outside the City, were expressly made for the purpose, a few having been used for beer or wine instead of bodies!

Many vaults were private, such as 'Lady Jersey's Vault' and 'Holden's Vault', both in St Bride's, Fleet Street, and in this same church there is a 'Doctor's Vault.' St Clement Danes and other churches have a 'Rector's Vault', and St Saviour's, Southwark, can boast of a 'Bishop's Vault'.

The bodies from under some of the City's churches which have been pulled down, were moved to others; the coffins from St Michael, Crooked Lane, were divided between St Edmund King and Martyr, and St Mary Woolnoth, and those that went to the latter place have had a second removal, the vaults having to be cleared out a few years ago. In many places there were vaults under the vestries, the adjoining schools, the almshouses, the sextons' houses, etc., and at Lambeth, among the places of interment closed by order in Council, was a 'vault under the station-house.' It is not unlikely that many of these will have, in time, to be cleared out. In some cases the coffins or remains have already been collected and re-interred in cemeteries, the one at Woking having been especially favoured. In the vaults, they are very liable to become a nuisance, and are far more dangerous to the living than the human remains under the plots of ground open to the air.

CHAPTER 11

GRAVEYARDS AS PUBLIC GARDENS

By the year 1877, seven disused burial-grounds in London had been converted into public gardens; those of St Botolph's, Bishopsgate, St George's in the East, and the Wesleyan graveyard adjoining (forming one ground), the additional ground for St Martin's in the Fields in Drury Lane, St. John's, Waterloo Bridge Road, and St Pancras' old churchyard, with the adjoining graveyard belonging to St Giles in the Fields (forming one ground). These may be called the five pioneer gardens. But St Botolph's was closed again for several years, and St Martin's for a short time, and St Pancras' and St Giles' had to have much more done to them before they became attractive open spaces, so the one that really stands out as the recreation ground that has had the longest existence is St George's, for this has been in constant use for twenty years.

The following is a list of those that have been laid out as recreation grounds and opened by the Metropolitan Public Gardens Association since the Spring of 1885:

1. St Bartholomew's Churchyard, Bethnal Green. E.

2. The East London Cemetery, E.

3. Holy Trinity Churchyard, S.E.

4. St Paul's Churchyard, Shadwell, E.

5. Spa Fields, Clerkenwell, E.C.

6. St John at Hackney Churchyard, E. (part of).

Churchyard of St. Botolph, Aldgate

7.   St Mary le Strand Ground in Russell Court, W.C.

8.   St James Churchyard, Bermondsey, S.E.

9.   Holy Trinity Churchyard, Mile End, E.

10. St Martin in the Fields, W.C.

11. St George's Churchyard, Camberwell. S.E.

12. St Dunstan's Churchyard, Stepney, E.

13. St Anne's Churchyard, Limehouse, E.

14. Trinity Chapel Ground, Poplar, E.

15. St Alphege Churchyard, Greenwich, S.E.

16. Seward Street Burial-ground, E.C.

17. St James' Churchyard, Ratcliff, E.

18. St Botolph's, Aldgate, E.

19. St Anne's Churchyard, Soho, W.

20. Shoreditch Old Ground, Hackney Road, E.

21. Christ Church Churchyard, Spitalfields, E.

22. All Saints' Churchyard, Poplar, E. (part of).

23. St Botolph's Churchyard, Bishopsgate, E.C.

24. St Katherine Coleman Churchyard, E.C.

25. St Olav's Churchyard, Silver Street, E.C.

26. Victoria Park Cemetery, or Meath Gardens, E.

27. Allhallows' Churchyard, London Wall, E.C.

28.St Mary's Churchyard, Bow, E. (part of).

29. St Peter's Churchyard, Walworth, S.E.

30. St Mary's, Churchyard, Woolwich, S.E.

There are now, within the metropolitan area, ninety burial-grounds actually dedicated to the public as recreation grounds, and being maintained as such under the *Open Spaces Act* of 1881, or by trustees, or under agreement with the vicar, etc., including four that are Board School playgrounds. To those who remember these places before they were converted, the transformation is wonderful. One Sunday in the year 1878, the Rev. H R Haweis told his congregation at St James', Westmorland Street, that in a hasty walk through their own parish burial-ground in Paddington Street, Marylebone, he had seen 'orange-peel, rotten eggs, cast-off hair-plaits, oyster-shells, crockery, newspapers with bread and meat, dead cats and five live ones' and that on the grave of one Elizabeth Smith 'in the very centre of the churchyard' he found 'twelve old kettles, two coal-scuttles, three old hats, and an umbrella.' Some of the congregation doubted it, but they went to look, and found it true!

There is a very charming little garden in Benjamin Street near Farringdon Road, which belongs to the parish of St John's, Clerkenwell. It was consecrated in 1755 by the Bishop of Lincoln acting for the Bishop of London, having been conveyed to trustees as an extra parochial gift to the parish by the will of Simon Michell, who died in

1750. After being closed for burials, it fell into the hands of a member of the Clerkenwell Vestry, and was covered with workshops and rubbish until the then Rector, the Rev. W. Dawson, instituted proceedings against him, secured the land, laid it out by public prescription in 1881 and maintained it at his own private expense. It is now in the hands of trustees, and the Holborn District Board of Works and the Clerkenwell Vestry contribute towards its upkeep.

Several other gardens in London have had a somewhat similarly checkered history. The burial-ground in Hackney Road belonging to Shoreditch has a quaint old building in it, once the parish watch-house, and used as a temporary hospital at the time of the cholera epidemic. A new gateway has been lately made at St James', Ratcliff, leading into the churchyard garden, erected as a memorial to the late vicar, the Rev. R K Arbuthnot, who spent very many years in the parish and died in harness.

Another quaint spot exists in the burial-ground of St George the Martyr, Bloomsbury, where stands a private gentleman's dissecting-room. Hackney Churchyard includes the ground surrounding the tower of the older church (St Augustine's), while Bermondsey Churchyard includes the cemetery of the Abbey. The little playground in Russell Court, Drury Lane, which was a graveyard attached to the parish of St Mary le Strand, is immortalised as 'Tom all alones' in Dickens' *Bleak House*. When the Association got hold of it, it was little other than a heap of decaying rubbish thrown from the surrounding houses, and the carcases of eighteen cats were removed at once. It is now an asphalted recreation ground and is often crowded with children using the swings and the seats. But it has lately lost its characteristic appearance, the surrounding houses have been pulled down, and it is at present 'opened out'.

It must not be supposed that there has been no opposition to the conversion of graveyards into public gardens. Many owners have refused to allow it, and from time to time – though the times are now getting very few and far between – letters have been written to the newspapers pointing out the danger of admitting the public to them. But the burial-grounds are there, in the midst of crowded streets, whether we like them or no, and they become far more wholesome when fresh soil is imported, good gravel paths made and the ground drained, and when grass, flowers, trees and shrubs take the place of rotting rubbish. A certain gentleman, somewhat well-known, wrote to the Times, arguing against the laying out of churchyards and saying that a 'blue haze' hung about a square in New York which was once a burial-ground. But no blue haze hangs about our gardens in London, and they are of the utmost value in all parts of the town.

On the other hand, every consideration should be shown for those whose objections to the transformation have been made on sentimental grounds. Conditions have been applied when a disused churchyard or burial-ground is being laid out and thrown open to the public; first, that any person interested in any particular tombstone has the right and the power to prevent such tombstone from being moved; second, that the inscriptions on the stones, and their exact positions in a ground to be laid out, are preserved in perpetuity in the office of the Registar of the Diocese, although the actual inscriptions themselves on the tombstones, whether a ground is closed or open, are daily becoming more defaced, and when it is closed there is no record of them and no guarantee that they may not be broken, shifted or stolen. Nor must it be imagined that the tombstones in all graveyard gardens have necessarily to be moved. It is only where they are standing so thickly that the ground cannot be laid out otherwise. In some places, such as Spa Fields, not a single gravestone existed when it came into the hands of the Association; in others, such as St Mary le Strand, there were only a few and these already on the walls, while in others, again, such as Holy Trinity, Rotherhithe, there were so few that it was not necessary to get a faculty to remove them, but they were left in place. There was one tombstone at All Saints', Poplar, which stands tall and solitary in the middle of a path, which could not be diverted because of other stones, and when the path was made, this particular monument was left in the very centre.

I think the very best way of disposing of tombstones is by putting them against the walls, even if it necessitates two or three rows. They are very dismal standing in groups, as at St James', Hampstead Road, and the wall of tombstones at St Luke's, Chelsea, is by no means attractive. Nor are the 'dome' and 'trophy' at St Pancras, to which I have already referred. In St John's Garden, Horseferry Road, they are cemented into an even row against the wall, and look as if they would last for ever.

I would not say that a converted graveyard is a better garden than a converted square, but there is something more interesting about it – it is so very human; and where there are monuments to notable persons, which naturally are undisturbed, they form something with an historical flavour about it which is attractive to look at. "Isn't it foine!" said a ragged little urchin to me on the day when that particular ground was thrown open to the public. He was simply bursting with delight at having a garden to go into. I answered that I thought it was. This reminds me of another little denizen of the slums, at Lincoln Inn Fields. He was inside – I had just left the ground after the opening ceremony. He peeped through the railings, overflowing with smiles; "You can come in, Miss," he said. I was not a Miss, but I thanked him for the information.

Apart from the moving of tombstones, there are many people who think it irreverent for a ground once used for burial ever to be used for recreation; they do not like the idea of walking about over the graves. This feeling is worthy of respect. It is found largely developed among the Jews, and has prevented them hitherto, from allowing any of their graveyards to be laid out as public gardens. There are other people – and I am thankful that I do not come across them – who would like our churches to be turned into theatres. They do far more harm to the cause of open spaces than do those who are slow to adapt themselves to modern ideas. But as far as my experience goes, I have found that the people who chiefly object to the conversion of burial-grounds into gardens are those who stay at home. They have in their mind's eye a picture of a well-kept cemetery, where burials take place every day, of a sweet village churchyard where the grass is soft and green and the graves peaceful and undisturbed. One of the last things that I should wish to see is a village churchyard turned into the village recreation-ground; and it was sad to find, as I did a short time ago, that a certain rural churchyard in West Middlesex was being used as a drying-ground for laundered clothes. But the London disused graveyards are SO different, that I believe it is only necessary to take these objectors (though they will never come) to point out to them the sinking graves, to help them pick their way so that they may avoid the dirty rubbish lying about, and the pitfalls into which they may stumble, in order to convince them that the ground, if turned into a public garden, would be treated with more reverence and in a more seemly manner. Then show them a gravyard garden; let them sit there for a bit to watch the people who come in and out, the men who have a brief rest in the middle of the day, the women who can snatch a few moments from their crowded and noisy homes, the big children with their 'prams' and the little children they have in charge – and the change in the minds of the objectors will be complete.

My impression is that amongst the London burial-grounds which are still closed and useless, there are fewer untidy ones than there used to be. The agitation that led to the laying out of eighty or ninety of them as public recreation grounds has also had a beneficial effect upon those which are not yet laid out. If this is the case, it is very satisfactory, and it is an indirect result of the labours of the members of the Metropolitan Public Gardens Association, and of others who have interested themselves in the matter, which should be a cause for thankfulness and encouragement.

CHAPTER 12

CEMETERIES STILL IN USE

B
esides the churchyards of Tooting, Plumstead, Lee and Eltham, that are still available for interments, and some others, such as Charlton and Fulham, where burials in existing graves or vaults are sanctioned on application to the Home Secretary, ten burial-grounds, which can hardly be called cemeteries, are still being used in London. These are the South Street or Garratt's Lane ground at Wandsworth, consecrated in 1808, where widows, widowers, and parents of deceased persons already interred there can be buried, and the Holly Lane ground in Hampstead, which was consecrated in 1812, and is occasionally used; the graveyard by the Friends' Meeting House in Stoke Newington, those in the convents in King Street, Hammersmith, and Portobello Road, and one in Newgate Gaol (to all of which I have already referred); and a burial-ground crowded with tombstones behind St Thomas' Roman Catholic Church in Fulham, where new graves are still dug, although there appears to be no room for more monuments, and although densely populated streets are on every side. The other three are Jewish grounds, one in Ball's Pond, and two in Mile End.

It will be noticed that when the Act was passed, under which the metropolitan burial-grounds were to be closed, seven of the new cemeteries were already in use, and while the burial-grounds were being closed, other cemeteries were being started. Several of the large cemeteries which have thus sprung into existence are just outside the metropolitan area, but the following are within the boundary of the County of London.

1. All Soul's Cemetery, Kensal Green

2. The South Metropolitan Cemetery, Norwood

3. St James' Cemetery, Highgate

4. Abney Park Cemetery, Stoke Newington

5. Brompton Cemetery, or the West London, or the London and Westminster Cemetery

6. All Saints' Cemetery, Nunhead

7. City of London and Tower Hamlets Cemetery, South Grove, Mile End

8. Lambeth Cemetery, Tooting Graveney

9. Charlton Cemetery

10 St Mary's Cemetery, Putney Lower Common

11. Woolwich Cemetery, Wickham Lane

12 Camberwell Cemetery, Peckham Rye

13. Greenwich Hospital Cemetery, Westcombe

14. Deptford Cemetery (St Paul's), Lewisham

15. St Mary's Roman Catholic Cemetery, Kensal Green

16 Lewisham Cemetery

17. St Mary's Cemetery, Battersea

18. Fulham Cemetery

19. Hammersmith Cemetery, Fulham

20. Lee Cemetery, Hither Green

21. Hampstead Cemetery, Fortune Green

22. Wandsworth Cemetery, Magdalen Road

23. Plumstead Cemetery

24. Greenwich Cemetery

Some of these cemeteries have been added to since they were first formed and, considering the rate at which they are being used, they will all need to be enlarged in a very few years, that is, if the present mode of interment continues to be the ordinary one.

It must not be imagined that land was secured for these cemeteries without difficulty. The inhabitants of the districts in which it was proposed to place them naturally petitioned aginst their formation. A huge scheme for securing ninety-two acres, the Roundwood Farm Estate, between Willesden and Harlesden, for the Great Extramural Cemetery Association, was opposed by the Middlesex magistrates and others, and was not sanctioned by the Secretary of State. Part of this site is now a public park. The parish of Kensington applied for permission to form a cemetery of thirty acres at Wormwood Scrubs, but eventually had to go as far out of London as Hanwell in order to secure a suitable plot. Unfortunately some public land was allotted. I believe that Norwood Cemetery was formerly part of Norwood Common, and Putney and Barnes Cemetery, the latter being just outside the boundary of London, are on Putney and Barnes Commons.

The cemetery at Tooting was once a meadow-land known as Baggery Mead, and for most of the others, farm land and fields were taken. Happily it would now be very difficult to acquire a piece of common land for any such purpose, as we know far better than we did, how to preserve our greatest treasures. How disastrous it would be if, when our village church-yards could no longer be used, the village greens were turned into burial-grounds!

In Norwood Cemetery, in 1851, only a single row of tombstones lined its paths; now there is row upon row behind them, the place seems to be entirely filled and 'yet there is room.' These grounds are all much alike, but Norwood is peculiar in containing a small parochial burial-ground belonging to St Mary at Hill, in the City (the Church of the Church Army), and another belonging to the Greeks. Most dwellers in London are acquainted with one or other of the cemeteries, some people finding pleasure in walking about in them, and sitting on the seats provided for visitors among the tombs; and they are, on the whole, well looked after and neatly kept. It is rather to be regretted that the custom of putting quaint and interesting epitaphs on the stones is so utterly a thing of the past; the monotonous texts do not take their place at all.

There is a special interest attached to Kensal Green Cemetery from its having been the first, but I think it is also the worst. The well-known author Mr Loftie describes it as 'the bleakest, dampest, most melancholy of all the burial-grounds of London.' I doubt if it is the dampest, though the soil is a heavy clay, for I think that the Tower Hamlets Cemetery is probably far damper. Nor is Kensal Green so overcrowded or untidy as Tower Hamlets, where gravestones are tumbling and lying about, apparently unclaimed and uncared for, among the dead shrubs and rank grass; it has also not quite so large a proportion of 'common' graves (for eight bodies or so), as there are in some other grounds, and the number of burials per acre has not been quite so enormous as, for instance, Tooting, Brompton or Abney Park. The last-named ground, when it had been opened fifteen years, was described in an official report as being 'a mass of corruption underneath', the soil being a 'damp, blue clay.' But Kensal Green is truly awful, with its catacombs, its huge mausoleums, family vaults, statues, broken pillars, weeping images and oceans of tombstones, good, bad and indifferent. I think the indifferent are to be preferred, the bad should not be anywhere, and the good are entirely out of place. It is also the largest in the Metropolis, and as the Roman Catholic ground joins it, there are in this spot, or there very soon will be, ninety-nine acres of dead bodies.

There are many sad sights in London, but to me there are few so sad as one of these huge graveyards. Not that the idea of the numbers of dead beneath the soil produces any thoughts of melancholy, but I feel inclined to exclaim with the disciples "To what purpose is this waste?" Can there be any more profitless mode of throwing away money than by erecting costly tombstones? They are of no use to the departed, and they are grievous burdens laid on the shoulders of succeeding generations. The only people who profit by them are the few marble and granite merchants, and a few monumental masons – and they might be better employed. The whole funeral system is an extravagant imposition, and has been for many years. It may be said that the heavy trappings, the plumes on horses and carriages, the scarves, the mourning dress, etc., are going out of fashion. I saw the other day a neat copy of the Funeral Service, bound in black leather, with a cross outside. On the fly-leaf was printed the name of the person to be buried, with the date of death, place of interment, etc. This book was given by the undertaker to each of those attending the funeral, and as the ceremony was conducted by a Nonconformist minister, who arranged it in accordance with his own individual predeliction, the little book was useless! I merely mention this as a specimen of the way in which the expenses of a funeral may be mounted up (see Appendix D). The rich lavish their money on costly, almost indestructible coffins, which would be far better to do without altogether, and on masses of flowers that die unseen, while the poor go into debt to buy mourning, which they often pawn before a month is over; and many a widow and family, who have a hard struggle to provide daily food, deny themselves the necessities of life, and sow the seeds of disease and want, in order to set up a tombstone or monument on a grave. And who sees it? A few people may occasionally go to Kensal Green Cemetery to look at the tomb of Princess Sophia or the monuments of other celebrities, but they are utterly spoilt by their surroundings. It is hardly possible to appreciate such memorials when they are so closely hedged in by others of all descriptions of stone, of all shapes and sizes, and in all types of architecture. And it is appalling to think of the amount of money that has been spent on these massive monuments. How many a church or chapel might have been built in a growing district; how many a beautiful old church now falling decay might have been restored; how many missionaries might have been sent to foreign lands; how many hospital beds might have been endowed; how many struggling families or sick members of the same, might have been given a holiday in the country or by the sea; how many open spaces might have been secured and laid out for the people; how many drinking fountains might have been erected; how many grants might have been made to voluntary schools or secular institutions for benefiting mankind; and how many objects of real beauty and antiquarian interest might have been preserved! It is impossible to give an answer to these questions – perhaps one would be sadder still if one could.

It has been the dying wish of very many of our best men that their bodies might be laid to rest in quietness, and without any undue expense or show. Unfortunately their wishes have not always been carried out. Sir John Mordern, who founded Mordern College or Almshouses for Decayed Merchants in Blackheath, left directions in his will that he should be interred in the chapel of the college 'without any pomp or singing boys, but decently.' I do not think the singing boys would have hurt him, but his wish to dispense with pomp was most praiseworthy. His funeral was made the occasion of a considerable ceremony but, as it took place at 9 o'clock in the evening, perhaps it was unaccompanied by such an institution as a champagne lunch.

I cannot conclude this division of my subject without an earnest appeal to those who are contemplating erecting a tombstone to the memory of a beloved relative or friend, to consider beforehand which is the wisest way to commemorate the departed – whether the simplest memorial is not after all the best; whether it may be better still to have none at all in a cemetery which is already overcrowded with monuments, and whether it is well to add indefinitely to the forests of practically imperishable gravestones which are gradually surrounding London and our other large towns.

CHAPTER 13

A FORECAST FOR THE FUTURE

Although the primary aim in presenting this book is the macabre one of directing the reader's attention to the possible presence of human remains still lurking 'beneath the floor', as it were, the following chapter, containing Mrs Basil Holmes' vision of the future, written in the 1890s, is included, raising the hypothesis – how do we, in the 21st century, think what things might be like, a hundred years from now? How right was she? How right would WE be?

I acknowledge a hesitation in writing this chapter, because there are many people who feel very strongly upon the subject of the disposal of the dead, and whose feelings I wish in no way to appear to treat with anything but the greatest consideration. The custom of burying the body has been in practice in England ever since Christianity was established, and so completely did burial take the place of burning that the latter expedient has never been formally forbidden, or, until 1884, even referred to in English law. It is well that this fact should be clearly understood, viz., that it is not illegal to dispose of a body by other means than by burial in the earth (unless it should be proved a public nuisance at common law), nor has it been illegal in England in the past, but it has merely not been the custom, 'inhumation' having been systematically practised for a thousand years.

But the earth does not want dead bodies; it is better without them, and there is a certain benefit to be derived from a moderate supply, and the most advanced crementionists advocate the use of the few remaining ashes as manure for some kinds of farm lands. Sir Henry Thompson, a crementionist worthy of every honour, has referred to the great increase there would be in the fish supply if burial at sea were generally practised, a plan approved of by some anti-crementionists. We have seen that churchyard water has been drunk for generations, and very bad it is. Churchyard poultry and churchyard mutton are also common enough, many a poor parson being glad to earn a few pounds in the year by allowing sheep to graze among the graves. This is all very well in some country places, but it used to be practised in London, and sheep have been actually killed by swallowing with the grass the poisonous products of the overfilled ground. In the Charterhouse graveyard there are some magnificent fruit-trees, such as are seldom seen in crowded towns; one of the Stepney pest-fields became a market-garden; while breweries and burial-grounds seem to be closely associated with each other.

But a question of paramount importance is how to stop the increase of cemeteries. Are we ever to allow England to be divided like a chess board into towns and burial-places? What we have to consider is how to dispose of the dead without taking so much valuable space from the living. In the metropolitan area alone, we have almost filled (and in some places overfilled) twenty-four new cemeteries within sixty years, with an area of about six hundred acres, and this is as nothing compared to the huge extent of land used for interments just outside the limits of the metropolis. If the cemeteries are not to extend indefinitely, they must in time be built on, or they must be used for burial over and over again, or the ground must revert to its original state as agricultural land, or we must turn our parks and commons into cemeteries, and let our cemeteries be our only recreation grounds – Heaven forbid!

I fail to understand how any serious-minded person can harbour the idea that burning the body can be any stumbling-block in the way of its resurrection, for the body returns 'earth to earth, ashes to ashes, dust to dust,' whether the process takes fifty years or fifty minutes. But many people have a horror of the notion – they know it is sanitary, but they think it irreverent. There are other alternatives, worthy of careful consideration. Some have advocated burial at sea; others, and among them Sir Seymour Haden, have pressed forward the advantages of using perishable coffins, wicker baskets, and the like – a suggestion as excellent as it is economical, for the sooner the earth and the body meet, the better it is. Perhaps, in this scientific generation, some one may invent a totally new method of disposing of the dead, which will commend itself both to those who advocate cremation and to those who dislike it. But that cremation is on the increase cannot be denied. Even Kensal Green Cemetery has now a 'Columbarium', which is an elegant name for pigeon-holes for cinerary urns, built in 1892, with forty-two little cupboards. Since the decision of Mr Justice Stephen in the case of Dr William Price in February 1884, it has been recognised as legal in England, and in the crematoriums at Woking and elsewhere, have been frequently used. But if the practice is to become at all general, it must be advocated by a different set of people. It has, to a certain extent, happened hitherto, that those who have been cremated have been more or less cremated with the advance school, those that consider themselves 'enlightened' Radicals, or Socialists, or persons of little or no professed religious views. This was not the case with the promoters of cremation, but it has been so with some of their disciples, or at any rate, many anti-cremationists think so. But I venture to think that cremation will not be taken up very largely until a few such men as the Archbishop of York and the Chief Rabbi pronounce in its favour. Then it would be necessary to have a crematorium in every cemetery.

It is foolish and useless to make previous provision for death, except by life insurance, a proper will, and other business-like arrangements. It is foolish to erect, as many have done, a tomb during lifetime, like the Miller's tomb in Highdown Hill, Sussex, to keep a coffin under the bed, or to have a picture of a skeleton always on the wall; such eccentric practices as that of a gentleman who died in a house by Hyde Park, and, at his wish, had his body kept in a coffin under a glass case on the roof of the house, are not to be admired. We can never forget that our life here will have its ending; our friends, companions, and neighbours are constantly leaving us, our daily paper has its obituary column, and surely no artificial method is needed to remind us of this fact. The utmost we need do, if we do not want our bodies to rest in the cemeteries, is to tell our friends that we wish to be cremated, or buried in perishable coffins, or quietly laid in some far-off rural spot,

A few word in closing, about the future of the disused burial-grounds in London. I think they are tolerably safe now. I have attempted to show how many there are still, closed and idle, or being used for a totally wrong purpose, between Hampstead and Plumstead, Hammersmith and Bow; but they are surely, if slowly, being reclaimed and changed, one by one, into places of rest and recreation for the living. The public mind has so far awakened to the necessity of securing all the breathing spaces which may be had, that the smallest corner of land in which interments can have been said to have taken place, now forms a subject of litigation if attempts are made to build on it. Preservation is the first step on the ladder, acquisition the next, while conversion crowns them all.

I can see no better fate for the disused graveyards than that they should become gardens or playgrounds. The churchyards must be gardens, and the unconsecrated grounds, detached from places of worship, will serve as playgrounds, many of them having to be reclaimed from their present use as builders' yards, cooperages, etc. Spa Fields, Clerkenwell, a burial-ground to the history of which I have already referred, is a typical London playground in the very centre of town, although surrounded by courts and streets with such rural names as Rosoman Street, Wood Street, Pear-tree Court and Vineyard Walk, grim reminders of what the district was like a hundred years or more ago. Exmouth Street, behind which this open space is situated, is worth a visit. I was there recently, one Monday afternoon. Trucks and stalls filled with all kinds lined the narrow road, and there seemed scarcely a square yard without a person on it. One woman was selling old garments, of which she had only about six, and these were spread out on the road itself – in the mud. A little further on I noticed a stall, where two women were making purchases of 'freshly-boiled horse-flesh at 2d a lb.' This was not cut up as for cats' meat, but was in large, dark-brown, shapeless-looking joints. In the middle of the street is the Church of the Holy Redeemer, a huge structure in imitation of an Italian church. It stands on the site of the Spa Fields Chapel, an old round building removed a few years ago, belonging to the Lady Huntingdon Connexion, which has a stone obelisk in front of it to the memory of Lady Huntingdon. Behind the church is an open space, which is nearly two acres in extent. Originally bought to trade as a tea-garden, the speculation failed, and the ground was used as a burial-ground, slightly lower fees being charged than in the neighbouring churchyards.

After being grossly over-crowded, it was closed for interments in 1853. For several years the space has been used as a drill-ground by the 3rd Middlesex Artillery and the 39th Middlesex Rifles, and in 1885 the Metropolitan Public Gardens Association entered into negotiations with the owner, the Marquis of Northampton, and he generously handed it over at a nominal rental for the purpose of a children's playground, and subsequently added to it half an acre of adjoining land. The Association drained it and carted a large amount of soil and gravel into it, and put up some gymnastic apparatus in the additional piece which was not a part of the burial-ground. The entrance is from Vineyard Walk, Farringdon Road. When I last visited the playground, although it was a chilly afternoon, a great many children were enjoying themselves, and some women were swinging their little ones. But after or between school-hours is the proper time to see it. Then it is crowded, and every swing and every rope, pole, bar, ladder and skipping rope is in use, and children are running about all over the open part of the ground.

It is a strange-looking place. On the north-west side is the unfinished apse of the Church of the Holy Redeemer, and on the south side is the parish mortuary, the presence of which does not seem to have any sobering effect upon the children. A playground such as Spa Fields is about as different from an ordinary village green, where the country boys and girls romp and shout, as two things with the same purpose can be. For the soft, green grass, you have gritty gravel; for the cackling geese who waddle into the pond, you have a few stray cats walking on the walls; for the pictureque cottages overgrown with roses and honeysuckle, you have the backs of little houses, monotonous in structure, in colour, and in dirt. And instead of resting underneath the trees, you must be content with a wooden bench bearing on its back the name of the association which laid out the ground. But it is only necessary to see the joy with which the children of our crowded cities hail the formation of such a playground, and the use to which they put it, to be convinced that the trouble of acquiring it, or the cost of laying it out, is amply repaid.

And can the dead beneath the soil object to the little feet above them? I am sure they cannot. Such a space as Spa Fields may never have been consecrated for the use of the dead, but perchance the omission is in part redeemed by its dedication to the living.

THE 364 BURIAL-GROUNDS WHICH STILL EXIST WHOLLY OR IN PART

T hey were there then, in 1895, but are they there now? And if not, what occupies the sites?

Hampstead

1. **St John's Churchyard**: 1½ acres in extent. It is full of tombstones, but very neatly kept, and although not handed over to any public authority, nor provided with seats, the gates are usually open.

2. **Burial-ground in Holly Lane**: 1¼ acres. This is still in use for interments and new graves are occasionally dug here. It was consecrated in 1812. It is tidily kept, and the gates are open whenever the gardener is there.

3. **Hampstead Cemetery**: 19½ acres : Open daily. First used in 1876. It is well kept, except for the part nearest to Fortune Green.

4. **The Tumulus, Parliament Hill Fields**: Excavated in 1894 by the London County Council and said to be an ancient British burial-place of the early bronze period. Railed around for its protection.

St Marylebone

5. **St Marylebone Episcopal Chapel-ground, High Street**: A third of an acre. This chapel was the parish church until 1816. The Churchyard is full of tombstones, closed and fairly neat.

6. **St Marylebone Burial-ground, Paddington Street, north side**: ¾ of an acre. A mortuary was built in it a few years ago. The ground was consecrated in 1772. It is closed to the public, but neatly kept and used as a garden for the inmates of the adjoining workhouse.

7. **St Marylebone (also called St George's) Burial Ground, Paddington Street, south side**: 2¼ acres. Consecrated in 1733, and very much used. Since 1886 it has been maintained as a public garden by the vestry and is well kept.

8. **St John's Wood Chapel-ground**: An additional burial-ground for the parish of Marylebone. 6 acres. The tombstones have not been moved, but the Marylebone Vestry maintains the ground as a public garden. It has a few seats in it and is neatly kept.

Paddington

9. **St Mary's Churchyard**: 1 acre. The tombstones have not been moved but the ground has been neatly laid out and is kept open by the vestry.

10. **The Old Burial Ground**: 3 acres. This adjoins St Mary's Churchyard and was laid out and opened as a public garden by the vestry in 1885. It contains the site of an older church, dedicated to St James.

Kensington

11. **St Mary Abbots Churchyard**: About 1 ¼ acres. The graveyard is smaller than it was 20 years ago because the present church is far larger than the original one, and recently a long porch or cloister has been added. It is neatly laid out but closed to the public.

12. **Holy Trinity Churchyard, Brompton**: 3½ acres. There are public thoroughfares through this ground, but they are railed off, and the churchyard is closed and has a neglected appearance.

13. **Brompton Cemetery**: also called West London Cemetery and London and Westminster Cemetery. 38 acres. First used in 1840. By 1889 upwards of 155,000 bodies had been interred there. It is crowded with tombstones and is in the midst of a thickly populated district.

14. **All Souls Cemetery, Kensal Green, partly in Hammersmith**: 69 acres. Open daily and neatly kept. Has been in use since 1833 and is crowded with tombstones and contains catacombs and numerous vaults and mausoleums.

15. **Burial-ground of the Franciscan Convent of St Elizabeth, Portobello Road**: This is a triangular grass plot, not above ¼ acre in size, in the garden behind the convent. It is surrounded by trees and is neatly kept. It is only used for the interment of nuns, of whom five have been buried here, the first in 1870, the last in 1893.

Hammersmith

16. **St Paul's Churchyard**: 1 acre. This is smaller than it used to be, the present church being larger than the old one, and a piece of the ground having been taken in 1884 to widen the road. It is neatly laid out and is often open, but not as a public recreation ground. It was consecrated in 1631 and frequently enlarged.

17. **St Peter's Churchyard, Black Lion Lane**: 1,800 square yards. Closed and untidy.

18. **New West End Baptist Chapel-ground, King Street**: ¼ of an acre, This is north and south of the chapel, the northern part having been encroached upon. Closed and neatly kept.

19. **Wesleyan Chapel Burial-ground, Waterloo Street**: The Chapel has been supplanted by a Board School and the playground is the site of the burial-ground. It is tar-paved, has a few trees in it, and is about 500 square yards in size.

20. **Friends' Burial-ground, near the Creek**: 300 square yards. This is on the north side of the Friends' meeting-house, and is closed but very neat. There are a few flat tombstones, and burials took place until about 1865.

21. **St Mary's Roman Catholic Cemetery, Kensal Green**: 30 acres. The first interment was in 1858 and it is now crowded with vaults, tombstones, etc. It is open daily and neatly kept.

22. **The Cemetery of the Benedictine Nunnery, Fulham Palace Road**: This is a small burial-ground in the garden. According to a report from the Home Office it is about 14 by 12 yards in extent. It was in use before 1829 but was closed for interment some years ago.

23. **The Cemetery of the Convent (Nazareth Home), Hammersmith Road**: This is at the extreme end of the garden under the wall of Great Church Lane. It is not more than 12 yards by 9 yards, and is used for the interment of the sisters, burials only taking place at considerable intervals. The ground here has been in use for upwards of 40 years.

Fulham

24. **All Saints' Churchyard**: Two acres or more. This is kept open during the summer months, and has seats in it, but the gravestones have not been moved, nor has the ground been handed over to any public authority for maintenance. It is neatly kept. No new graves are dug in it, but where the rights can be proved, certain old vaults are still occasionally used.

25. **St Mary's Churchyard, Hammersmith Road**: Size ½ of an acre. This ground is closed, but fairly tidy. Several of the tombstones have been moved.

26. **St John's Churchyard, Walham Green**: ½ of an acre. There are only a few tombstones on the north side of the church and none on the south side, and the ground is closed and appears neglected.

27. **St Thomas' Roman Catholic Churchyard**: 2,600 square yards. This ground was closed by order in Council in 1857, but only partially, for new graves are still being dug in it, in the midst of a densely populated district of new streets. The gate is usually open.

28. **Lillie Road Pest Field (the orchard of Normand House)**: The site of this orchard, then 4 acres in extent, was used extensively for burials at the time of the Great Plague of 1665. Lintaine Grove now occupies part of it, and a row of houses in Lillie Road. Only about 6 acre is still unbuilt on, at the corner of Tilton Street, and this is offered for sale.

29. **Fulham Cemetery**: 12½ acres. First used in 1865. Open daily.

30. **Hammersmith Cemetery in Fulham Fields**: 16½ acres. First used in 1869. Open daily.

Chelsea

31. **St Luke's Churchyard (the old church on the Embankment)**: ¼ of an acre. This ground is closed and neglected.

32. **St Luke's Church (the new church in Robert Street)**: 2¼ acres. This ground was consecrated in 1812, and contains vaults and catacombs. It was laid out as a public garden and is maintained by the Chelsea Vestry.

33. **Old Burial-ground, King's Road**: ¾ of an acre. It was given to the parish of Chelsea by Sir Hans

Sloane, consecrated in 1736, and enlarged in 1790. It is laid out as a garden for the use of the inmates of the adjoining workhouse. Fragments of an old chapel and graveyard have been found here.

34. **Chelsea Hospital Graveyard, Queen's Road**: 1½ acres. This ground was used for the interment of the pensioners. It is closed, but neatly kept.

35. **All Souls Roman Catholic Burial-ground, Cadogan Terrace**: 1 ½ acres. The adjoining chapel (St Mary's) was consecrated in 1811. The ground is closed and full of tombstones.

36. **Moravian Burial-ground, Milman's Row**: The part actually used for interment is fenced in and closed. It is neatly kept, the tombstones being very small flat ones. It belongs to the congregation of the Moravian Church in Fetter Lane, E. C. and was closed by order in Council about 8 years ago.

37. **Jewish Burial-ground, Fulham Road**: ½ of an acre. It belongs to the Western Synagogue, St Alban's Place, S.W., and was first used in 1813. It is closed to the public except between 11 and 4 on Sundays.

St George's, Hanover Square

38. **St George's burial-ground, Mount Street**: 1¼ acres. Laid out as a public garden, and beautifully kept by the vestry. The ground dates from about 1730, but there are very few tombstones.

39. **St George's Burial-ground, Bayswater Road**: Laid out by the vestry, the gravestones having been placed round the walls. The approaches to this ground are its chief drawback, and it is not visible from any public road. One entrance is through the chapel facing Hyde Park, and the other is in a mews. It is about 5 acres in extent.

St. Margaret's and the Abbey Churchyard about 1750

Westminster (St Margaret and St John)

40. **The Churchyard of Westminster Abbey**: What remains of the extensive burial-ground which once occupied this site is the piece of land on the north side of the Abbey, and the cloisters.

41. **St Margaret's Churchyard**: This was laid out as a public garden and forms one ground with the Abbey churchyard. It is well kept up by the burial board of the parish. The size of the churchyard, with the ground used for interments which belongs to the Abbey, is about 2 ¼ acres.

42. **Christ Church Churchyard (also called St Margaret's burying-ground), Victoria Street**: This church was a chapel of ease to St Margaret's. The adjoining graveyard has had a vicarage built

in it. What remains is 7000 square yards in size, closed, with flat tombstones and grass.

43. **St John the Evangelist Churchyard, Smith Square**: This churchyard used to extend, at the beginning of the century, for some distance on the south side of the church, but was encroached by the road. Now all that remains is a very small, bare enclosure, not a ¼ acre in size, railed in round the church.

44. **Additional ground for St John's Parish, Horseferry Road**: Walled in, in 1627, and very much used, especially for the burial of soldiers. It is 1 ½ acres in size, and has been laid out as a public garden. It is neatly kept by the vestry, and much frequented.

45. **Vincent Square**: 8 acres. This is what remains of the Tothill Fields pest-field. It is the playground of Westminster School, and some buildings have been erected in it. A stone-paved yard in Earl Street is said to be the site of the plague pits.

46. **Millbank Penitentiary Burial-ground**: 432 square yards in size. In 1830-31 there was an average of 14 interments per annum, but at times it was more used. The site of this graveyard will be preserved when the space which used to be occupied by the prison is built on.

47. **Knightsbridge Green**: Victims of the Plague from the leper hospital and elsewhere were buried here. A grassy closed triangle opposite Tattersalls.

St Martin's in the Fields

48. **St Martin's Churchyard**: One third of an acre. This is stone paved, has trees and seats in it supplied by the Metropolitan Public Gardens Association, and it maintained by the vestry.

49. **Additional Ground in Drury Lane**: Less than ¼ of an acre. Laid out as a public garden and

now maintained by the vestry. It is well-kept, and contains some gymnastic apparatus for the use of children. Also called the Tavistock burial-ground.

St James's Church, Westminster

50. **St James's Churchyard, Piccadilly**: ½ of an acre. This is a dreary ground, and might be made very attractive. The part where most burials took place is considerably raised above the rest. The yard on the north side of the church is entirely paved with stones. In the upper part, tombstones form the walks, the walls, etc. One gate is often unlatched.

51. **St James's Workhouse-ground, Poland Street, off Oxford Street**: The workhouse was built up on a 'common cemetery' where, at the time of the Plague, many thousands of bodies were interred. A small part of it was kept as the workhouse burial-ground, but this has now disappeared, and all that is left of the original ground used for interments is the garden or courtyard of the workhouse. It is a pleasant recreation ground for the inmates, and is well supplied with seats, being about a ¼ of an acre in extent.

The Strand

52. **St Mary le Strand Churchyard**: At the west end of the church, about 200 square yards in size, closed and not well kept.

53. **Additional Ground, Russell Court, Catherine Street**: It is 430 square yards in size. It is probable that few grounds in London were more over-crowded with bodies than this one, which was entirely surrounded by the backs of small houses. When closed in 1853 it was in a very disgusting and unwholesome condition, and it continued to be most wretched until the Metropolitan Public Gardens Association asphalted it in 1886. It is maintained as a children's playground by the London County

Council. This is the scene of 'Tom all alone's' in Dicken's *Bleak House*. There are six gravestones against the wall.

54. **St Clement Danes' Churchyard**: This is now ¼ of an acre in extent, having been curtailed when the Strand was altered. It is closed.

55. **Additional Ground, Portugal Street**: This was called the 'Green-ground' and was crowded with bodies. A corner of King's College Hospital was built upon the ground. The remaining piece is nearly ½ of an acre in size, between the hospital and Portugal Street. It is now the entrance drive and a grass plot. It is neatly kept, with some seats and trees in it, and is used solely by the hospital.

56. **St Paul's Churchyard, Covent Garden**: It is ¾ of an acre in extent. Given by the Earl of Bedford in 1631. It is closed and very neat, the tombstones forming a flat paved yard round the church, while the rest of the ground is turfed.

57. **St Ann's Churchyard, Soho**: It is estimated that in this small ground and the vaults under the church 110,240 bodies were interred during 160 years. It was laid out by the Metropolitan Public Gardens Association in 1892, and is maintained as a recreation ground in very good order by the Strand District Board of Works.

58. **The Churchyard of the Chapel Royal (St Mary's), Savoy**: This is a ¼ of an acre in extent. The ground was much used for the interment of soldiers. It belongs to Her Majesty Queen Victoria, as Duchess of Lancaster, and was laid out as a public garden at the cost of the Queen, the Earl of Meath, and others. It is well maintained by the parish.

St Giles in the Fields

59. **St Giles' Churchyard**: Nearly an acre in size. This ground being originally consecrated by a Roman

Catholic, was much used by the poor Irish. It was enlarged in 1628 and at various subsequent dates, and was very much over-crowded, and it occupies the site of an ancient graveyard attached to a leper hospital. It has been laid out as a public garden, and is maintained by the St Giles' District Board of Works. The brightest part of the ground is north of the church, and this is only opened at the discretion of the caretaker.

Holborn

60. **Additional Ground for St John's, Clerkenwell, in Benjamin Street**: This land, which is nearly a ¼ of an acre in extent, was consecrated in 1775. It was laid out as a public garden ten years ago, and is maintained by trustees with help from Holborn District Board of Works and the Clerkenwell Vestry. Very well kept.

61. **Charterhouse Square**: This garden is part of the site of a burial-ground dating back to 1349, when Sir Walter de Manny purchased from St Bartholomew's Hospital 13 acres of land, known as the Spittle Croft, for the burial of those who died in the plague of that time. In 20 years 50,000 bodies were interred there. In 1371 the Carthusian Monastery was built upon it. The Pardon Churchyard was the space of three acres acquired a year later, to which the plague ground was added. This Pardon Churchyard survived longer, being used for suicides and executed people. Charterhouse Square is 1¼ acres.

62. **The Old Charterhouse Graveyard**: In 1828 to 1830, when the present Pensioners' Court and other buildings were erected, part of this ground was built on; but part exists in the courtyard on each side of the Pensioners' Courts, being about one third of an acre in extent. All the open land has been used at one time or another for burials.

63. **The New Charterhouse Burial-ground**: When
     the above ground was done away with, a smaller
     piece in the north was set aside for the interment of
     the pensioners. This remains still, and is very neatly
     kept. There are a few gravestones on the wall and
     splendid fruit trees. It is about a ¼ acre in extent.

Clerkenwell

64. **St James' Churchyard**: It is about ¾ of an acre.
     This ground was purchased in 1673, enlarged in
     1677, and is now laid out as a public garden and
     maintained by the vestry.

65. **Additional Ground, Bowling Green Lane
     (called St James' Middle Ground)**: This was
     leased by the parish, with the adjoining 'Cherry
     Tree' public house, in 1775, for 99 years. It is ¾
     of an acre in size and is situated at the corner of
     Rosoman Street and Bowling Green Lane. The
     London School Board secured it when the lease ran
     out, and it is now the playground of the Bowling
     Green School.

66. **The Burial-ground of St James's, Pentonville
     Road**: This was formed as an additional ground for
     the parish of St James, Clerkenwell. It is nearly an
     acre in extent, full of tombstones and very untidy,
     but the Metropolitan Public Gardens Association
     has undertaken to convert it into a public garden.

67. **St John's Churchyard**: What remains of this exists
     between the church and St John Street, a narrow
     strip about 320 square yards in extent, closed and
     paved with tiles and tombstones. Its laying out by
     the Metropolitan Public Gardens Association is in
     hand.

68. **Spa Fields Burial-ground, Exmouth Street**:
     Originally a tea-garden, afterwards a burial-ground,
     managed by a private individual. It is the property
     of the Marquis of Northampton, is about 1 ¾
     acres in extent, and in the evenings is occasionally

used as a volunteer drill-ground. In 1885 the Metropolitan Public Gardens Association laid it out as a playground, and the London County Council mantains it.

St Pancras

69. **St Pancras Burial-ground, Pancras Road**.

70. **St Giles in the Fields Burial-ground, Pancras Road**: These two grounds now form one garden, about 6 acres in extent, maintained with much care for the use of the public by St Pancras Vestry. St Giles' ground dates from 1803, but the other is much older. In 1889 part of the St Pancras ground was acquired under a special Act by the Midland Railway Company. This part was, in 1791, assigned to the French immigrants, and many celebrated Frenchmen and Roman Catholics were buried there. Part of it has not actually been built upon, as the railway travels over it on arches. There are many high stacks of tombstones in the garden, and a 'trophy' and a 'dome' of headstones, 496 in number, which were taken from the part acquired by the railway.

71. **St Martin's in the Fields Burial-ground in Pratt Street**: This is of 1 ¾ acreage. It was consecrated in 1805 and is now a well-kept public garden under the control of the St Pancras Vestry. A part appears to have been appropriated as a private garden for the almshouses and as a site for a chapel and other buildings.

72. **St James's Burial-ground, Hampstead Road**: This belongs to the parish of St James, Piccadilly. It was laid out as a public garden in 1887, and is maintained by the St Pancras Vestry, a large slice at the east end having been taken off for public improvements. The remaining portion measures about 3 acres.

73. **St Andrew's Burial-ground, Gray's Inn Road**: it is 1¼ acres in size. This ground belongs to the parish of St Andrew, Holborn, adjoins the Church of Holy Trinity, and is maintained as a public garden by the St Pancras Vestry. It is well-kept, except for a railed-off piece south of the church, which is a sort of lumber-room.

74. **The Burial-ground of St George's, Bloomsbury**

75. **The Burial-ground of St George the Martyr, Bloomsbury**: These are out of Wakefield Street, and together form one large public garden maintained by the St Pancras Vestry, and are very well-kept. A part of the latter, which was consecrated in 1714, is still closed. Each ground is 1 ¼ acres in extent. There are vaults under the church in Hart Street.

76. **Whitfield's Tabernacle Burial-ground, Tottenham Court Road**: Some-what less than ½ an acre. The London County Council opened it as a public garden in February, 1895. It is said that in 97 years upwards of 30,000 bodies were interred in this ground.

77. **Wesleyan Chapel-ground, Liverpool Street, King's Cross**: An untidy little closed yard at the west end of the chapel containing two tombstones and much rubbish, and measuring about 225 square yards.

78. **St James's Cemetery, Highgate**: 38 acres in extent. First used in 1839. In 50 years 76,000 bodies had been buried here. It is in two portions and situated on a steep slope. Open daily.

Islington

79. **St Mary's Churchyard**: It is 1½ acres in size. This ground was enlarged in 1793 and was laid out as a public garden in 1885. It is maintained by the vicar and churchwardens.

80. **Additional Ground round the Chapel of Ease in Holloway Road**: It is 4 acres in extent. This is also laid out as a public garden, and is beautifully kept by the Islington Vestry.

81. **Burial-ground of St John's Roman Catholic Church, Duncan Row**: ½ an acre. A strip at the northern end of this ground is railed off with some tombstones in it, the remainder being tar-paved and used as a playground for the boys' Roman Catholic School.

82. **Islington Chapel Ground, Church Street (also called Little Bunhill Fields)**: The original chapel was built in 1788, and had a small graveyard. In 1817 the Rev. Evan Jones bought the garden of No, 5 Church Row, and added it to this graveyard, the whole ground being nearly 1 acre in extent. It is now in several divisions; part is a yard belonging to the General Post Office, and the other parts are let and sold as builders' yards or are vacant.

83. **Maberley Chapel-ground, Ball's Pond Road**: Now called Earlham Hall. The ground is about 270 square yards, between the chapel and the road. It is closed and bare.

84. **Jewish Burial-ground, Ball's Pond**: 1 ¼ acres. This belongs to the West London Synagogue, is very neatly kept, and is still in use. It is full of very large tombstones.

St Luke's

85. **St Luke's Churchyard, Old Street**: In two parts. The size of the whole ground is nearly 1 ¾ acres. The piece round the church is closed and full of large altar tombs, ivy being planted most profusely. There is a great deal of rubbish in it. The part on the north side was laid out as a public garden in 1878, and is maintained by the vestry.

86. **The Poor-ground, Bath Street**: This was originally larger than it is now. It was consecrated in 1662 for the parish of St Giles, Cripplegate, and called the pest-house ground. After 1732, when St Luke's parish was formed, it was used by that parish. Now it is neatly laid out and used as a recreation ground by the patients of the St Luke's Asylum. It is ¼ acre in extent.

87. **Bunhill Fields**: 5 or 6 acres. This was originally two grounds, the southern part having been intended for burials in the Great Plague but, not being used, was let by the Corporation to a Mr John Tyndall, who carried it on as a private cemetery. Subsequently the northern part was added, and the whole ground extensively used for the interment of dissenters. The Corporation maintains it as a public garden, but the tombstones have not been moved, and only the gates at the eastern end are generally open.

88. **Wesleyan Chapel-ground, City Road**: ½ acre. The part in front of the chapel is neatly kept, but the part behind is closed and not so tidy. Wesley himself was buried in a vault here.

89. **The Friends Burial-ground, Bunhill Row**: Acquired in 1661, many times added to, and chiefly used by the Friends of the Peel and Bull-and-Mouth divisions. In 1840 a school was built on it. The existing portion is about ½ an acre in size, and is neatly kept as a private garden, but the remainder was used as the site for a Board School, a coffee palace, houses and shops, including the Bunhill Fields Memorial Buildings, erected in 1881.

90. **St Bartholomew's Hospital Ground, Seward Street**: One third of an acre in size. This was used for the interment of unclaimed corpses. After being closed, it was let as a carrier's yard until it was laid out as a public playground by the Metropolitan Public Gardens Association in 1891. It is maintained by St Luke's Vestry.

91. **Cripplegate Poor-ground, Whitecross Street**: It was called the 'upper churchyard' of St Giles, and was first used in 1636. It was very much overcrowded, the fees being low. A part of the site is occupied by the church and mission-house of St Mary, Charterhouse, erected in 1864, and only a very small courtyard now exists between these buildings, with a very large vault.

92. **The City Bunhill (or Golden Lane) Burial-ground**: It is 1 ¼ acres in extent. This was the site of a brewery and was set aside for burials in 1833. About one third of it is in the City. It is now divided; one part of it is in the occupation of Messrs. Sutton and Co., carriers, and is full of sheds and carts, the greater part being roofed in, and the southern part has the City Mortuary and Coroner's Court on it. What is unbuilt upon is a neat, private yard between these two buildings. It was closed for burials in 1853.

Shoreditch

93. **St Leonard's Churchyard**: 1½ acres in size. Maintained as a public garden by the Shoreditch Vestry. It is, I believe, partly in Bethnal Green.

94. **Old Burial-ground, Hackney Road**: ½ an acre. This has an ancient watch-house in it, which was subsequently used as a cholera hospital. In 1892 the Metropolitan Public Gardens Association laid it out as a public garden, and it is maintained by the Burial Board.

95. **Holywell Mount Burial-ground**: Behind St James' Church, Curtain Road, which occupies the site of a theatre of Shakespeare's time. The ground is very old, and was much used at the time of plagues, and many actors are buried there. There is only about one third of an acre left, the greater part having been used as the site for a parish room, and this is a timber yard approached from Holywell Row.

96. **St Mary's Churchyard, Haggerston**: 1½ acre in extent. This is maintained by the Shoreditch Burial Board as a public garden, open during the summer. It was laid out by the Earl and Countess of Meath in 1882.

97. **St John's Churchyard, Hoxton**: 1¼ acres. Also maintained by the Shoreditch Burial Board, and laid out by the Earl and Countess of Meath.

98. **Jewish Burial-ground, Hoxton Street**: ¼ acre. This belongs to the United Synagogue, and was used from 1700 till 1795. There is no grass, but many tombstones, and someone is sent four times a year to clear away the weeds, etc. It is not a tidy ground.

Hackney

99. **St John's at Hackney Churchyard**: 6 acres in size. This includes an older ground, attached to the original church of St Augustine, of which the tower still remains. Part of the churchyard is laid out as a public garden, and is neatly kept by the Hackney District Board of Works, but the newer part to the south of the church is still full of tombstones and rather untidy grass. The newest part of all, the 'poor ground', which is at the extreme southern end, is laid out for the use of children.

100. **West Hackney Churchyard, Stoke Newington Road**: Nearly 1 ½ acres. This was consecrated in 1824 and laid out as a garden in 1885. It is maintained by the Hackney District Board of Works.

101. **St Barnabas's Churchyard, Homerton**: ¾ acre. This ground is not open, but a good deal of care is shown in its management. In 1884 the Easter offerings were devoted to its improvements, and many tombstones were then laid flat.

102. **St John of Jerusalem Churchyard, South Hackney**: About ¾ of an acre. This was consecrated in 1831. It is full of tombstones and the grass is not well-kept, but it is usually open for people to pass through. It was closed for burials in 1868.

103. **Wells Street Burial-ground**: This contains the site of the original South Hackney Church. It was laid out as a public garden in 1885 and is very neatly kept by the Hackney District Board of Works. Nearly ¾ of an acre.

104. **Independent Chapel Burial-ground, Mare Street (also called St Thomas' Square Burial-ground)**: Two thirds of an acre. Laid out in 1888 and maintained by the Hackney District Board of Works, who paid £100 for a passage to join this ground with No. 103, one caretaker managing both of them. It is very bright and neat. The ornamental shelter occupies the site of a previous building.

105. **Baptist Chapel-ground, Mare Street**: About 500 square yards at the back of the chapel. There are several tombstones tumbling about and the ground is very untidy.

106. **New Gravel Pit Chapel-ground, Chatham Place, attached to the Unitarian Church**: ¾ acre in size. This is full of tombstones and is fairly tidy. The gate is usually open, the chapel-keeper living behind the chapel, and having a green-house and fowl-house, etc. in the ground.

107. **Retreat Place**: A garden in front of twelve almshouses, founded in 1812 'for the widows of Dissenting ministers professing Calvinistic doctrines.' Samuel Robinson, the founder, and his wife, are buried in the middle of the garden.

108. **Jewish Burial-ground, Grove Street**: 2¼ acres. This belongs to the United Synagogue and was purchased in 1788. It is closed and full of erect tombstones, and has some trees and flower-beds near the entrance.

Stoke Newington

109. **St Mary's Churchyard**: ¾ of an acre. A very pretty ground round the old church, but not laid out or opened.

110. **Friends Burial-ground, Park Street, Stoke Newington, adjoining the meeting house**: ¾ acre. This was bought in 1827 and enlarged in 1849. It is still in use and neatly kept, but not open to the public.

111. **Abney Park Cemetery**: 32 acres in extent. First used in 1840. Neatly kept and open daily, being chiefly used by the Dissenters, It is crowded with tombstones.

Bethnal Green

112. **St Matthew's Churchyard**: About 2 acres. This was consecrated in 1746 and was much over-crowded. A mortuary was built in it some years ago. There are vaults under the schools as well as the church. It is closed, but negotiations are on foot respecting its conversion into a garden.

113. **St Peter's Churchyard, Hackney Road**: ¼ of an acre. This churchyard is maintained as a public garden by the vicar, who opens it during the summer months, There are not many tombstones.

114. **St Bartholomew's Churchyard, near Cambridge Road**: Nearly an acre. This was laid out by the Metropolitan Public Gardens Association in 1885, and is maintained by the London County Council. It is very much appreciated.

115. **St James the Less Churchyard, Old Ford Road**: Over an acre. Closed and considerably below the church. It contains about ten tombstones, and several cocks and hens live in it. It is bare and damp.

116 **Providence Chapel Burial-ground, Shoreditch Tabernacle, Hackney Road**: Was built on the site

of the chapel. Part of the graveyard exists as a tar-paved yard or passage by the Tabernacle, with four tombstones against the walls.

117. **Victoria Park Cemetery**: This is maintained as a public park by the London County Council, having been laid out in 1894 by the Metropolitan Public Gardens Association. It was formed in 1845 and used for forty years. Before being laid out it was a most dreary, neglected-looking place; the soil is a heavy clay, and there used to be large wet lumps lying about all over the ground. At a burial in 1884 the clerk brought a handful of earth out of his pocket to throw upon the coffin instead of using a nearby wet lump. Now it is a bright, useful little park, and is called Meath Gardens.

118. **Peel Grove Burial-ground (also called North-East London Cemetery, Cambridge Heath or Road Burial-ground and Keldy's Ground)**: According to a return in 1855 it was four acres in extent, but now there is hardly one acre. It is in the occupation of J. Glover and Sons, dealers in building materials, and it is full of wood, pipes, etc. There are some sheds in it. It was a private ground formed 100 years ago, and was very much crowded. The late Metropolitan Board of Works saved the existing part from being built over. Before its present use it was often let out for shows, fairs, etc.

119. **Gibraltar Walk Burial-ground, Bethnal Green Road**: Another private ground, formed about 100 years ago. It belongs to a lady who lives in the house which opens into it and who has let pieces of it as yards for the shops and houses around. It is full of shrubs, trees and weeds, and covered with rubbish, and is about ¾ of an acre in size.

120. **Jewish Burial-ground, Brady Street**: This existed 100 years ago, and belongs to the United Synagogue. I believe it is about 4 acres. It is crowded with upright stones, and there are no properly made

paths, but it is covered with neglected grass. Part of it is higher than the rest, the soil having been raised and the ground having been used a second time. This was the 'Strangers' portion.

Whitechapel

121. **St Mary's Churchyard**: ¾ of an acre. This is a very old churchyard and was very much overcrowded with graves. It is maintained by the rector as a garden, but a charge of 1d. is made for entrance. It is neatly laid out.

122. **Additional Ground, Whitechapel Road, entrance in St Mary's Street**: This was called the work-house burial-ground, the workhouse having been built in 1768 upon a former graveyard, and this piece to the north of it having been set aside for interments and consecrated in 1796. The workhouse site was built upon some years ago, and the burial-ground became the playground of the Davenant Schools, one of which, the one facing St Mary's Street, was built on it. In the order for closing it, dated May 9th 1853, it is called the Whitechapel Workhouse and Schools Ground. It is difficult to say exactly how far east the burial-ground extended, but from the Ordnance map and some older plans it would appear that the recent addition to the school in Whitechapel Road has been built in the burial-ground. In 1833 the size was given as 2,776 square yards, but it was stated that in 1832, one hundred and ninety six cholera cases were interred in an adjoining piece of ground. This is probably what is now used as a stone-yard, with carts in it.

123. **Christ Church Churchyard, Spitalfields**: 1¾ acres. Laid out as a public garden by the Metropolitan Public Gardens Association in 1892, the assocation having undertaken to maintain it for five years.

124. **St Peter ad Vincula Churchyard, in the Tower**:
This, with the vaults under the Royal Chapel, was
used for the interment of distinguished prisoners.
It is part of the great courtyard and is about 525
square yards in extent (see Appendix D).

125. **Holy Trinity Church, the Minories**: A burial-
ground possibly dating back to 1348. It has been
added to the roadway of Church Street, some posts
showing its boundaries. It was about 302 square
yards in extent. Part has been built upon (see
Appendix D).

126. **Aldgate Burial-ground, Cartwright Street**:
This belongs to the parish of St Botolph, Aldgate,
and was consecrated in 1615. At the beginning of
this century it was covered with small houses, the
Weigh House being built on it in 1826. The rookery
(slum), was cleared by the Metropolitan Board of
Works, and Darby Street was made, gravestones
and human remains being then discovered. The
Metropolitan Public Gardens Association informed
the Board of the former existence of the burial-
ground, with the result that what remained of the
burial-ground was not built upon, but was made
into an asphalted playground, about an eighth of
an acre in extent, for the children of the adjoining
block of tenements.

127. **German Lutheran Church, Little Alie Street**: A
small yard exists at the back of the church. Closed.

128. **Friends' Burial-ground, Baker's row**: Very
nearly an acre. This belonged to the Friends of
the Devonshire House division, who acquired it in
1687. It is leased by the society to the Whitechapel
District Board of Works, who maintain it as a public
recreation ground. It is well laid out and well kept,
being chiefly used by children.

Friends' Burial-ground in Whitechapel

129. **Mile End New Town Burial-ground, Hanbury Street**: This adjoins the chapel, and extends from Hanbury Street to Old Montague Street. A school and other buildings have been erected on it, and all that is left is a paved yard about 250 square yards in size, on the west side of the chapel.

130. **Sheen's Burial-ground, Church Lane**: A private ground, immensely used. It seems to have been at one time used by the congregation of the Baptists in Little Alie Street, and was then called 'Mr. Brittain's burial-ground.' If so, it existed in 1763. After being closed for burials it was used as a cooperage (barrel-making), and now it is Messrs. Fairclough's yard and full of carts and sheds, etc. A new stable was built in 1894, but the London County Council declined to prevent its erection. The size of the ground is about ½ an acre.

131. **The London Hospital Burial Ground**: In a plan of 1849 the whole of the southern part of the enclosure is marked as a burial-ground, which

would be 1 ½ acres in extent. It was closed on 25th November 1853, but at the hospital it was stated that corpses were interred there after 1859, though not after 1864. Since then the medical school, the chaplain's house, and the nurses' home have been built in it. The remaining part of the ground is used as a garden and tennis-lawn for the students and nurses.

St George's in the East

132. **St George's Churchyard**: Dates from about 1730. The wall between this ground and the next one was taken down in 1875 and the two grounds were laid out as a public garden. They are maintained by the vestry, and although in a densely crowded district, are beautifully kept. The size of the whole garden, consisting of the two graveyards, is about three acres.

133. **St George's Weslyan Chapel-ground, Cable Street**: This forms one garden with the above.

134, **New Road Congregational Chapel-yard, Cannon Street Road, between Lower and Upper Chapman Streets**: This was a much-used burial-ground, part of which has been covered with sheds and houses. What is left is about a third of an acre in extent. The chapel was bought in 1832 and became Trinity Episcopal Chapel, and was subsequently removed and its site used for the new building of Raine's School. The burial-ground is in three parts, viz., the playground of the school, a cooper's yard belonging to Messrs. Hasted and Sons, and a carter's yard of Messrs. Seaward Brothers.

135. **Danish Burial-ground, Wellclose Square**: The Danish (or Mariners') Church has been supplanted by the Schools of St Paul's, London Docks, and the whole of the garden is neatly laid out and used as a private ground for the people who look after the schools, the nursery, etc. There are no tombstones

now, and it is possible that only an enclosure round the church was used, like the railed-in enclosure in Prince's Square.

136. **Swedish Burial-ground, Prince's Square**: Round the Eleanor Church, over ½ an acre in size. It is very neatly laid out and well kept, and contains many tombstones.

137. **Ebenezer Chapel Burial-ground, St George's Street**: This was described in 1839 as being very much overcrowded with corpses. The chapel has been used as a school, but is now deserted; the small yard on the southside of it is used as a timber yard, and closed. About 220 square yards.

138. **Congregational Chapel-ground, Old Gravel Lane**: 140 square yards. Closed, bare and untidy, with two gravestones against the wall.

139. **Baptist Burial-ground, Broad Street, Wapping**: Mentioned by Maitland in 1756, and shown on cartographer Rocque's plan. The chapel has gone but part of the adjoining yard exists as a small yard belonging to a milkman. Before he bought it, it was the parish stone-yard. It is about 200 square yards in size. I have little doubt that this is a burial-ground.

140. **Roman Catholic Burial-ground, Commercial Road**: The tombstones are flat and the ground is used as a private garden for the priests. It is about half an acre in extent.

Limehouse

141. **St Anne's Churchyard**: Consecrated in 1730 and since enlarged, but in 1800 a piece was cut off to become part of Commercial Road, the bodies being removed south of the church. Laid out as a public garden by the Metropolitan Public Gardens Association in 1887, it is now maintained by the London County Council. It is neatly kept, except the passage to the Mortuary.

142. **St Paul's Churchyard, Shadwell**: ¾ of an acre in size. Consecrated in 1671 but used before that as a pest-field for Stepney. Laid out by the Metropolitan Public Gardens Association in 1886, and now maintained and kept in good order by the London County Council.

143. **St James's Churchyard, Ratcliff**: Nearly one acre in extent. Laid out as a garden by the Metropolitan Public Gardens Association in 1891, and maintained by the vicar.

144. **St John's Churchyard, Wapping**: 600 square yards. Consecrated in 1617. This ground used to be very low and full of water. It is closed and fairly tidy, having many large altar tombs in it.

145. **Additional ground opposite St John's Church**: Rather over ½ an acre. This was one of the Stepney pest-fields. It is closed but tidy. There are quantities of tombstones in this ground, many of them which seem to be falling to pieces, and an unusual number of trees and flowering shrubs.

146. **Friends Burial-ground, Brook Street, Ratcliff**: 800 square yards. This is approached through the house on the south side of the meeting-house. It was acquired by the Society of Friends in 1666 or 1667, the land being originally copy-hold, but enfranchised in 1734 for £21. It is neatly kept and has four small upright stones.

147. **Brunswick Wesleyan Chapel-ground, Three Colt Lane**: Approached via a passage at the back of the chapel. It is about 450 square yards in size, and is used as a private garden. There are vaults under the chapel and three tombstones. It is said that about one thousand corpses were buried here, the last interment taking place in 1849.

Mile End Old Town

148. **St Dunstan's Churchyard, Stepney**: About six acres, or rather more. At the time of the Great Plague

of 1665, about one hundred and fifty corpses were interred here daily, and several extra grounds were provided for the parish. It was laid out as a public garden in 1887 by the Metropolitan Public Gardens Association. It is a most useful and shady ground, and is very neatly kept by the London County Council.

149. **Stepney Meeting House Burial-ground, White Horse Street (also called the Almshouse Ground and Ratcliff Workhouse Ground)**: Size half an acre. There are many tombstones and the ground is fairly tidy. The gate is generally open, as the entrance to the almshouses is through it.

150. **Holy Trinity Churchyard, Tredegar Square**: ¾ of an acre. Laid out by the Metropolitan Public Gardens Association in 1887, and maintained by the London County Council. The gravestones have not been moved, and some of the graves are still occasionally used, though no new ones are dug.

151. **Wycliffe Chapel Burial-ground, Philpott Street, Stepney**: ¾ of an acre in extent. This ground dates from 1831 and is behind the chapel and the Scotch church. It is full of tombstones, closed and untidy. The historian Chadwick divides it into a part belonging to the chapel and a larger part belonging to the Scotch church, but it appears to be all one now, and it is in the hands of the elders of Wycliffe Chapel.

152. **Globe Road Chapel Burial-ground, also called Mile End Cemetery**: The chapel is now Gordon Hall and belongs to Dr Stephenson of the Children's Homes. The burial-ground is in private hands. The ground was very much overcrowded with corpses and there were vaults under the chapel, the school and the sexton's house, but all the part south of the chapel was taken by the Great Eastern Railway Company. The existing piece is about 670 square yards in extent, is closed

and most untidy, quantities of rubbish lying about among the tombstones.

153. **East London Cemetery, Shandy Street, also called the Beaumont Burial-ground**: 2¼ acres. This was much crowded. It was laid out as a playground by the Metropolitan Public Gardens Association in 1885 and is maintained by the London County Council.

154. **Burial-ground of the Bancroft Almshouses, Mile End Road**: The People's Palace is on the site of the almshouses, and part of the burial-ground has been merged into the roadway on the east side of the palace. St Benet's Church, Hall and Vicarage were built in this ground, the church being consecrated in 1872. Three pieces still exist, in all less than ½ an acre; one is in the vicarage garden, another is open to the road, and the northern part is closed and roofed over, forming a little yard where flag-staffs, etc. are stored. The open part is also a store-yard, having heaps of stones in it, besides much rubbish. There are gravestones against the wall.

155. **Stepney Pest-field**: Many acres to the south of the London Hospital were used for interments at the time of the Plague, and the Brewers' Garden and the space by St Philip's Church are, according to some authorities, part of the site originally called Stepney Mount. At the Home Office it is believed that there have been no burials in the ground around St Philip's, nor have there since it was St Philip's churchyard; but I think that there were, long before the first St Philip's Church and the Brewers' Almshouses existed. The Brewers' Garden is open to the public on the charge of 1d.

156. **Jewish Burial-ground, 70 Bancroft Street**: About 1,650 square yards in size. This ground belongs to the Maiden Lane Synagogue, and is crowded with upright tombstones. The grass is

neglected. Burials still take place. It is a densely populated district.

157. **Jewish Burial-ground, Alderney Road**: 1 acre. Formed in 1700, enlarged in 1733. Belongs to the United Synagogue. The tombstones are upright, and they are not so thick as in most of the Jewish grounds, while the grass is kept more neatly.

158. **Jewish Burial-ground, Mile End Road**: This ground is nearly ¾ of an acre in extent and is at the back of the Beth Holim Hospital. It belongs to the Spanish and Portuguese Jews, the tombstones are flat, there are several trees, and the ground is very neatly kept. Part of the graveyard (where it is said that there have been no interments) has some seats in it, and is used by the patients of the hospital as a garden.

159. **Jewish Cemetery, Mile End Road**: 4 ¾ acres. This belongs to the Spanish and Portuguese Jews and is still in use. The gravestones are flat ones and low altar tombs, and the ground is neatly kept, although very bare.

Poplar

160. **All Saints' Churchyard**: The size, with that part which is used for the burial of cholera victims on the other side of the road, is 4 acres. The northern part of the churchyard was laid out by the Metropolitan Public Gardens Association in 1893, the rector having undertaken to maintain it for a few years. It is much appreciated and well kept.

161. **St Matthia's Churchyard**: This church was the chapel of the East India Dock Company and is sometimes called the Poplar Chapel. It is 1 ¼ acres in extent. It is in the middle of the Poplar Recreation Ground, is closed and fairly tidy. There are many tombstones.

162. **St Mary's Churchyard, Bow**: 2,716 square yards. This is in two portions, the eastern one is closed, but the western one has been laid out by the Metropolitan Public Gardens Association and is provided with seats, the rector maintaining it.

163. **St Mary's Churchyard, Bromley-by-Bow, or Bromley Street St Leonard**: This churchyard is 1 ¾ acres in size and is closed, but is very neatly kept up by the parish, and has some tombstones of artistic value in it. Its opening as a public garden is under consideration.

164. **Baptist Chapel-ground, Bow**: one third of an acre. Part of this ground is railed off as a private garden, the rest is used as a thoroughfare by the school children. There are several tombstones, some of which have been put against the walls.

165. **Trinity Congregational Chapel-ground, East India Dock Road**: one third of an acre. This was laid out in 1888 as a public garden, the minister of the chapel maintaining it. On his removal from the district, it was closed and was not re-opened.

166. **Roman Catholic ground, Wade's Place**: 1,300 square yards. This belonged to St Mary's Roman Catholic Church in Finsbury Circus, Moorfields, and was chiefly used for the poor Irish. It was a very damp and unwholesome ground. It is now used as a playground for the adjoining Roman Catholic school.

167. **City of London and Tower Hamlets Cemetery (partly in Mile End)**: 33 acres. First used in 1841. By 1889 247,000 corpses had been interred here, many being buried in common graves (i e containing more than one body, sometimes as many as eight or nine in number). It is still in use and open daily, a regular ocean of tombstones, many of which are lying about, apparently uncared for and unclaimed; in fact, most of the graves, except those at the edges of the walks, look utterly neglected, and parts of the

All Saints, Wandsworth, about 1800

ground are very untidy. It is situated in a densely populated district.

Wandsworth

168. **All Saint's Churchyard, High Street**: ¼ acre. This is closed and is much more tidy at the eastern end than the western end.

169. **East Hill Burial-ground, Wandsworth Road**: ½ acre. This ground was consecrated in 1680 and many French Huguenots were buried in it. It is closed and fairly tidy.

170. **Garratt Lane Cemetery, South Street**: It is 1¾ acres in extent. This was consecrated in 1808. It is closed to the public, and closed for interments with the exception of widows, widowers, and parents of deceased persons already interred there. It is maintained by the Wandsworth Burial Board.

171. **Friends Burial-ground, High Street**: 400 square yards. This is attached to the meeting-house, is closed and very neatly kept. There are a few upright gravestones.

172. **Baptist Burial-ground, North Street**: an untidy little closed yard with no tombstones in it, and neglected grass. The chapel now belongs to the Salvation Army. I doubt if it was much used for burials, but, at any rate, there was one interment in it, in 1834. It is about the same size as the Friends' ground.

173. **Independent Burial-ground**: This is now a small tar-paved yard adjoining Memorial Hall, which was built on the site of an old chapel or school-house. There are a few trees.

174. **St Mary's Churchyard, Putney**: ½ an acre. Closed and neatly kept.

175. **Putney Burial-ground, Upper Richmond Road**: 1 acre. This was a gift to the parish from the Rev. R. Pettiwand, and consecrated in 1763. It was laid out in 1886, but the tombstones were not moved, and many of them are dilapidated brick altar tombs. It is maintained for the public by the Putney Burial Board.

176. **St Nicholas' Churchyard, Lower Tooting**: 2 acres in size. This is still in use. It is open daily and kept in good order.

177. **Lower Tooting Chapel-ground**: 231 square yards behind the chapel (Congregational in the High Street) and about 30 square yards in front. There are some tombstones. The chapel dates from 1688 and was founded by Daniel Defoe.

178. **St Leonard's Churchyard, Streatham**: 1¼ acres. The present church dates from 1831, but the churchyard is at least a hundred years older. It is closed for burials and well planted with trees, flowers and grass. The gates are sometimes open.

179. **St Paul's Churchyard, Clapham, in the Wandsworth Road**: 1½ acres. This is closed, and very full of tombstones. It is maintained by the

Clapham Burial Board, but it is in a rather jungly condition.

180. **Union Chapel-ground, Streatham Hill**: About 500 square yards. This is a neat little garden between the chapel and the schools, both of which have been rebuilt, the schools in 1878. There is a row of tombstones against the walls. It is generally closed.

181. **Wandsworth Cemetery**: 12 acres. First used in 1878. Open daily.

182. **Lambeth Cemetery, Tooting Graveney**: First used in 1854. Open daily.

183. **Putney Cemetery**: 3 acres in extent. First used in 1855. This is an encroachment on the common.

Battersea

184. **St Mary's Churchyard**: ¾ of an acre. The laying out of this ground is under consideration.

185. **St George's Churchyard, Battersea Park Road**: ¾ acre. This is closed and in a very neglected condition. There are not many gravestones.

186. **Battersea Cemetery, Bolingbroke Grove**: 8½ acres. First used in 1860. Open daily.

Lambeth

187. **St Mary's Churchyard**: ½ an acre. A very old ground, enlarged in 1623 and 1820. It is very neatly laid out and the gates are left open, although there are no seats in it.

188. **Additional ground in High Street (also called Paradise Row burial-ground)**: 1 ½ acres. Given to the parish by Archbishop Tenison, and consecrated in 1705. It was laid out in 1884 by the Lambeth Vestry, who maintain it efficiently.

189. **St John's Churchyard, Waterloo Bridge Road**: An acre in size. This was laid out as a garden and playground in 1877, and is well kept by the Lambeth Vestry.

190. **St Mark's Churchyard, Kennington**: 1¾ acres. This is closed and full of tombstones, but is neatly kept.

191. **Regent Street Baptist Chapel-ground, Kennington Road**: A little ground at the back of the chapel with a few tombstones and one great vault in it.

192. **Esher Street Congregational Chapel-ground, Upper Kennington Lane**: About 480 square yards, closed and very untidy.

193. **St Matthew's Churchyard, Brixton**: 2 acres in size. This dates from 1824. It is closed but neatly kept.

194. **Denmark Row Chapel-ground, Coldharbour Lane**: This is been partly built on, and there is now only a small yard behind the chapel.

195. **Stockwell Green Congregational Chapel-ground**: ¼ acre, or rather more. This is behind the chapel, and is a particularly neglected and untidy graveyard.

196. **St Luke's Churchyard, Norwood**: 1 acre. This dates from 1825. It is tidily kept, except the part near the station. The gate is generally open. The gravestones are still in place.

197. **Congregational Chapel-ground, Chapel Road, Lower Norwood**: About ½ an acre behind the chapel. It is closed, and has grass and a few tombstones in it.

198. **Norwood Cemetery**: 40 acres. First used in 1838. Open daily and fairly well kept. It is crowded with tombstones, and it includes a Greek cemetery, and a burial-ground belonging to the parish of St Mary at Hill, each about 550 square yards in size.

Camberwell

199. **St Giles's Churchyard**: 3¼ acres. It was enlarged in 1717, 1803, and 1825. Closed, full of tombstones, and not well kept.

200. **St George's Churchyard, Well Street, Camberwell**: The church was consecrated in 1824, the ground being given by Mr John Rolls. The churchyard measures about an acre, and was laid out in 1886 by the Metropolitan Public Gardens Association. It is maintained by the vestry. A mortuary has been built on it.

201. **Dulwich Burial-ground, Court Lane, the graveyard of God's Gift College**: Size 1½ roods. This ground dates from about 1700. It is closed and very neatly kept.There are several large altar tombs in it, and it is a most rural and picturesque spot.

202. **Wesleyan Chapel-ground, Stafford Street, Peckham**: 336 square yards. The chapel is now a school, the burial-ground being the playground, a paved yard.

203. **Friends Burial-ground, Peckham Rye**: About 470 square yards in area. This ground was purchased in 1821, is behind the meeting-house in Hanover Street, and has some small flat gravestones in it, and is closed. It is most beautifully kept, with neatly mown lawns and a border of flowers.

204. **Camberwell Cemetery, Forest Hill Road**: 29½ acres. First used in 1856. Open daily.

205. **Nunhead Cemetery (All Saints)**: 50 acres in extent. First used in 1840. Open daily.

Newington

206. **St Mary's Churchyard**: 1¼ acres. This was enlarged in 1757 and 1834, and is now maintained as a public garden by the burial board, the freehold being vested in the rector. It is well laid out.

207. **St Peter's Churchyard, Walworth**: 1 ¾ acres. This is also maintained as a public garden by the Newington Burial Board, having been laid out by the Metropolitan Public Gardens Association, at the

sole cost of the Goldsmith's Company, and opened in 1895.

208. **Sutherland Congregational Chapel-ground, Walworth**: This is close to St Peter's, about 300 square yards in size, and closed. It has been somewhat encroached on by the school, which was enlarged in 1889. A few tombstones exist in the passage on the north side of the chapel and in the ground at the back. It is fairly tidy.

209. **York Street Chapel-ground, Walworth**: About 700 square yards at the rear of the chapel and not visible from the street. It is closed and full of tombstones, but is to be laid out.

210. **East Street Chapel-ground, Walworth**: About 400 square yards, with one small tombstone in it. It is closed and very untidy.

211. **St John's Episcopal Chapel-ground, Walworth**: In 1843 it was estimated as measuring 6,400 square yards. The chapel is in Penrose Street, and is now the workshop of a scenic artist, the front wall having been heightened for the purpose of advertising the *South London Press*. The burial ground is approached from Occupation Road, Manor Place, the railway going across it on arches, and it is now the vestry store for carts, manure, gravel, etc. An adjoining plot is the site for the baths and washhouses. This ground is in danger of being encroached upon, and new bays for dust and other erections of the sort are often built on it.

212. **New Bunhill Fields, Deverell Street, New Kent Road (also called Hoole and Martin's)**: ¼ of an acre. This was a private speculation, and was most indecently overcrowded. Between 1820 and 1838 ten thousand corpses were buried here, the vault under the church containing 1,800 coffins. The ground was close in 1853 and it then became a timber-yard. The chapel now belongs to the Salvation Army, but the burial-ground is still

'Deverell's Timber-yard' and is covered with high stacks of timber. There are many sheds in it, and iron bars, etc.

St George the Martyr

213. **St George's Churchyard, Borough**: This is about an acre in size, and is maintained as a public garden by the rector and churchwardens, having been laid out in 1882. It is much used.

214. **St George's Recreation-ground, Tabard Street (the Lock burial-ground)**: Rather over ¼ acre. This was originally the burial-ground of the Lock Hospital which was pulled down in 1809, a portion of the site of the hospital and ground having been before then, consecrated as a parish burial-ground. It was chiefly used for pauper burials and was crowded with bodies. It is now a neat public garden, laid out by the vestry in 1887, and in the possession of the rector and churchwardens of St George's.

215. **Chapel Graveyard, Collier's Rents, Long Lane**: This is about 620 square yards in extent, and is on the north side of an old Baptist chapel, which now belongs to the Congregational Union. The ground dates from before 1729 and is closed. There are a few tombstones and grass, but it is not very well kept.

St Saviour's, Southwark

216. **St Saviour's Churchyard**: This ancient ground has been often enlarged and curtailed, and at times was used as a market place. What now exists is about ½ an acre on the south side of the church, which at present is under restoration.

217. **Additional ground for St Saviour's, called the College Yard or St Saviour's Almshouses Burial-ground, Park Street**: This existed before 1782; size ¼ of an acre. The London, Brighton and South Coast Railway goes over it on arches, and it is

now the storeyard of Messrs. Stone and Humphries, builders. Most of it is roofed in, but is not actually covered with buildings.

218. **Additional ground for St Saviour's, called the 'Crossed Bones', Redcross Street**: This was made, at least 250 years ago, 'far from the parish church' for the interment of the low women who frequented the neighbourhood. It was subsequently used as a pauper ground, and was crowded to excess. Nevertheless two schools were built on it. The remaining piece is about 1,000 square yards. It has frequently been offered for sale as a building site, and has formed the subject for much litigation. It is made a partial use of by being let for fairs, swings, etc. It was sold as a building site in 1883, but not having been used by 1884, the sale was declared null and void under the *Disused Burial Grounds Act.*

219. **Christ Church Churchyard, Blackfriars Bridge Road**: 1½ acres. This dates from about 1737 and has been enlarged. An infant school was built on it. It is closed and not laid out.

220. **Deadman's Place Burial-ground**: Deadman's Place is now called Park Street. This ground was originally used for the interment of large numbers of victims of the Plague. Then it became the graveyard of an adjoining Independent chapel, and was extensively used for the interment of ministers, being a sort of Bunhill Fields for South London. Now it is merely one of the yards over which trucks run on rails in the middle of the large brewery belonging to Messrs. Barclay and Perkins; about ½ an acre in extent. It existed as a burial-ground in 1839, but not, I believe, in 1841.

221. **Baptist Burial-ground, Bandy Leg Walk (subsequently called Guildford Street)**: There was such a ground in 1729. In 1807 there existed the Saviour's Workhouse, with a burial-ground on

the east side of it which, from its position, may have coincided with the Baptists' ground, and what is now left of the burial-ground is a garden or courtyard, about 1,000 square yards in size, between the new buildings of the Central Fire Brigade Station, Southwark Bridge Road, and an old house behind them. It is entered through the large archway.

St Olave's

222. **St Olave's Churchyard, Tooley Street**: a stone-paved yard, 634 square yards in extent, between the church and the river. Closed.

223. **Additional ground to St Olave's and to St John's, Horselydown, near St John's Church**: About ½ an acre, with a few tombstones in it. This was laid out in 1888, being chiefly asphalted, and is maintained as a recreation-ground by the Board of Works for the St Olave's District. It is well-used and neatly kept.

224. **St John's Churchyard, Horselydown**: Nearly two acres, it was laid out as a public garden in 1882 and maintained by the St Olave's Board.

225. **St Thomas's Churchyard**: This does not adjoin the church, but is behind the houses opposite. Size about 787 square yards. It belongs to St Thomas's Hospital and is used as a private garden by a house in St Thomas' Street.

226. **St Thomas's Hospital Burial-ground, St Thomas' Street**: Part of this ground has been covered by St Olave's Rectory and Messrs. Bevington's leather warehouse. The remaining piece measures about 1,770 square yards, and is an asphalted tennis-court and garden for the students of Guy's Hospital, the building in it being the treasurer's stables. It belongs to St Thomas's Hospital and is leased to Guy's.

The Remains of Bermondsey Abbey about 1800

227. **Butler's Burial-ground, Horselydown**: This was made about 1822, the entrance being in Coxon's (late Butler's) Place, and was 1,440 square yards in size. It is now Zurhoorst's cooperage and is full of barrels. A small piece, which I believe was part of the burial-ground, is a yard belonging to a builder named Field. There were vaults running under four dwelling houses. These still exist, and are under the houses next to the entrance to Mr Field's yard.

Bermondsey

228. **St Mary Magdalen's Churchyard**: Rather over 1½ acres. This ground was enlarged in 1783 and 1810, and contains the remains of an ancient cemetery belonging to the Bermondsey Abbey. It is maintained as a public garden by the vestry, the rector reserving certain rights. It is well laid out, and forms a most useful and attractive garden.

229. **St James's Churchyard, Bermondsey, Jamaica Road**: 1¾ acres in extent. It was extensively used as a drying-ground for laundered clothes when the

Metropolitan Public Gardens Association secured it in 1886, and laid it out as a garden. It is maintained by the vestry.

230. **Roman Catholic Ground, Parker's Row**: The land was given for the purpose in 1833 or 1834. The ground between the church and the road measures about 300 square yards, and was very much overcrowded. It is closed and untidy, with no tombstones. Burials also took place in the garden, which is used as a recreation ground for the schools, and is neatly kept.

231. **Southwark Chapel Graveyard (Wesleyan), Long Lane**: 900 square yards in area. This is on the west side of the chapel, which dates from 1808. It is closed, and contains a few gravestones and a hen coop.

232. **Guy's Hospital Burial-ground, Nelson Street**: This ground is nearly two hundred years old, and is rather over ½ an acre. Since being closed it has been let as a builders' yard. The Bermondsey Vestry is now negotiating for its purchase as a recreation ground.

233. **Friends Burial-ground, Long Lane**: ¼ of an acre. This was bought in 1697 for £120. It was closed in 1844, but in 1860 a large number of coffins, etc. were brought here and interred, when Southwark Street was made, and the Worcester Street burial-ground annihilated. It is being laid out for the public and will be maintained by the Bermondsey Vestry, who have it on lease from the Society of Friends. There are no gravestones in it.

234. **Ebenezer Burial-ground, Long Lane**: This adjoins the above ground, and it is hoped that it may eventually be added to the garden. It was formed about a hundred years ago. It originally belonged to the Independent Chapel in Beck Street, Horselydown, and subsequently to the trustees of Ebenezer Baptist Chapel. There is a 'minister's

vault' in the centre. It is closed and untidy, and is 220 square yards in extent.

Rotherhithe

235. **St Mary's Churchyard**: ¾ of an acre. This is closed, except on Sundays. It is full of tombstones and is kept in good order.

236. **Additional ground in Church Street**: 1¼ acres. This is also only open on Sundays, and is fairly tidy.

237. **Christ Church Churchyard, Union Road**: 700 square yards. This is closed, and there are no tombstones on the north side of the church. The south side is rather untidy except round the grave of General Sir William Gomm, who gave the ground for the church (being the Lord of the Manor), where there is a patch of good grass and flowers.

238. **All Saints' Churchyard, Deptford Lower Road**: Nearly one acre in extent. This land was given by Sir William Gomm in 1840, and was in use for 17 years. It is closed, and wooden palings separate it from the ground in front of the church. It is not well kept.

239. **Holy Trinity Churchyard, near Commercial Docks Pier**: About 1 acre. Consecrated in 1838. This ground was also only used for 20 years; a part of it is railed off for the vicarage garden, where probably no interments took place. It was laid out by the Metropolitan Public Gardens Association in 1885, and taken over by the London County Council in 1896. It is a very attractive, shady garden.

Greenwich

240. **St Alphege Churchyard**: Enlarged in 1716, 1774, and 1808. Size 2,740 square yards. This was laid out by the Metropolitan Public Gardens Association in

1889, and is maintained by the Greenwich District Board of Works. There are no seats in it.

241. **Additional ground, separated from the above by a public footpath**: This ground is 2½ acres, and was consecrated in 1833. It was laid out in 1889 by the Metropolitan Public Gardens Association, and is maintained by the Greenwich Board of Works. There are plenty of seats, and it is well used and neatly kept.

242. **St Nicholas Churchyard, Deptford**: ¾ of an acre. This is closed and full of tombstones, but fairly tidy.

243. **Additional ground, Wellington Street**: ¾ of an acre. This ground, belonging to the parish of St Nicholas, was laid out in 1884 by the Kyrle Society, and it is very well kept up by the Greenwich Board of Works, who have lately acquired a piece of adjoining land to be joined to the recreation ground.

244. **St Paul's Churchyard, Deptford**: 2½ acres. This is vested in the rector and maintained by the Deptford Burial Board. The gravestones have not been moved, but there are a few seats in the ground, which is open to the public.

245. **Baptist (Unitarian) Chapel Burial-ground, Church Street**: This touches the above, and is about ¼ of an acre. It is closed, the railings and gravestones are broken, and there is a quantity of rubbish lying about.

246. **Friends Burial-ground, High Street, Deptford**: About 360 square yards extent. This is behind the meeting-house, and closed. It is neatly kept and contains only one gravestone.

247. **Congregational Chapel Burial-ground, High Street, Deptford**: About 400 square yards. This is closed, but neatly laid out, and there are gravestones against the wall.

248. **Congregational Chapel-ground, Greenwich Road**: ¼ of an acre or slightly less. This dates from 1800. The gate is often open and the gravestones are flat on the ground or against the walls, but it is a bare, uninteresting-looking ground.

249. **Congregational Chapel-ground, Maze Hill, Greenwich**: A rather neglected looking ground, in Park Place, with several flat tombstones, about 500 square yards in size.

250. **Greenwich Hospital Burial-ground adjoins the Royal Naval Schools**: Measures about 4 acres. An inner enclosure is full of tombstones, but the outer part has only some monuments in it. It is very well kept, with splendid trees and good grass, and the gate from the school playground is generally open.

251. **Greenwich Hospital Cemetery, in Westcombe**: This is nearly 6 acres in size, and was first used in 1857.

Lewisham

252. **St Mary's Churchyard**: 2 acres. Laid out as a public garden in 1886, and maintained by the Lewisham District Board of Works.

253. **St Bartholomew's Churchyard, Sydenham**: ¾ of an acre. Closed for interments. This is beautifully kept and is a very pretty ground. The gates are generally open, but there are no seats.

254. **Deptford Cemetery**: 17 acres in area. First used in 1858. By 1889 50,000 corpses had been interred there.

255. **Lewisham Cemetery**: 15 ½ acres in size, of which 4 are reserved and let as a market garden. First used in 1858.

256. **Lee Cemetery, in Hither Green**: 10 acres, of which 4 are in reserve; these are open daily. First used in 1873.

Plumstead

257. **St Nicholas' Churchyard**: Still in use for burials, but under regulation. It is open daily, and measures about 4 acres.

258. **Woolwich Cemetery, Wickham Lane (partly outside the boundary of Plumstead)**: 32 acres. First used in 1856. Open daily.

259. **Plumstead Cemetery, Wickham Lane**: 32½ acres. First used 1890. Open daily.

Lee

260. **St John the Baptist Churchyard, Lee, Eltham**: 3 acres in extent. This is also in use, but under regulation, and is open daily.

261. **St Margaret's Churchyard**: Still in use, open daily, and very neatly kept. It is about 1½ acres in extent.

262. **The Old Churchyard**: This is opposite to St Margaret's and contains the ruins of the old church. It is full of old tombstones and neatly kept. It is generally open but has no seats in it.

263. **St Luke's Churchyard, Charlton**: ½ an acre. This is full of tombstones and closed, but very neatly kept. Burials occasionally take place in existing vaults, but in each case permission has to be obtained from the Home Secretary.

264. **St Thomas's Churchyard, Charlton, on the borders of Woolwich**: Nearly an acre. This churchyard was in use for burials in 1854, when it was put under regulation.

265. **Morden College Cemetery, Blackheath**: ¼ of an acre. Closed and neatly kept. Contains about 80 tombs, the college was founded about 1695.

266. **Charlton Cemetery**: 8 acres. First used in 1855. Open daily.

267. **Greenwich Cemetery**: 15 acres. Open daily.

Woolwich

268. **St Mary's Churchyard**: More than three acres. In a fine situation overlooking the river. Laid out as a public garden by the Metropolitan Public Gardens Association, at the cost of Mr Passmore Edwards, and opened in May 1895. It is maintained by the Woolwich Local Board.

269. **Enon Chapel-yard, High Street**: 112 square yards. A tar-paved and closed yard, with some tombstones against the wall.

270. **Union Chapel Graveyard, Sun Street**: One third of an acre. This is closed. There is a very bad fence round it, and it looks uncared for. Negotiations are on foot to secure it for the public.

271. **Salem Chapel-yard, Powis Street**: 300 square yards. Eighteen or twenty years ago the London School Board took the chapel and adopted it as a school. It is now the infant school, other buildings have been added, and the graveyard is a tar-paved passage used as a playground.

272. **Wesleyan Chapel-yard, William Street**: ¼ of an acre. Here a school building has evidently encroached upon the burial-ground. There are several tombstones, and it is fairly tidy, the gate being often open.

273. **Roman Catholic Ground, New Street**: This also has probably been encroached upon. What now exists is a yard, ¼ of an acre in size, between the school and the Roman Catholic Church, with three graves in one enclosure in the middle. The gate is open during school hours.

The City – Burial-grounds which are now public recreation grounds

274. **St Paul's Cathedral Churchyard**: Used as a burial-place since Roman times. It includes the Pardon Churchyard, the burial-grounds for the

parishes of St Faith and St Gregory, and a piece
allotted to St Martin's, Ludgate. Size, 1½ acres.
Maintained by the Corporation. Laid out in 1878-
1879.

275. **St Botolph's Churchyard, Aldersgate Street**.

276. **Additional Ground for Christ Church,
Newgate Street**.

277. **Additional Ground for St Leonard's, Foster
Lane**; These three form together one public garden,
rather more than ½ acre in extent. Very neatly kept
up with parochial funds.

278. **St Olave's Churchyard, Silver Street**: site of
the burned church.

279. **Allhallows' Churchyard, London Wall.**

280. **St Katherine Coleman Churchyard, Fenchurch
Street.**

281. **St Botolph's Churchyard, Aldgate**: ¼ of an
acre. Four grounds laid out by the Metropolitan
Public Gardens Association (see Appendix D).

282. **St Botolph's Churchyard, Bishopsgate**:
size nearly ½ an acre. This was laid out by the
Metropolitan Public Gardens Association, but the
entire cost was borne by the parish.

283. **St Botolph's, Billingsgate, upper burial-
ground, Botolph Lane.**

284. **St Mary Aldermanbury Churchyard**.

285. **St Sepulchre's Churchyard, Holborn** (see
Appendix D).

286. **St Bride's Churchyard, Fleet Street**: Five
small grounds laid out with the assistance of the
Metropolitan Public Gardens Asociation.

287. **Additional ground for St Dunstan's in the
West, in Fetter Lane**: Asphalted and used as a

playground for the Greystoke Place Board School. Some tombstones remain in an enclosure at the edge. 4,750 square feet in area.

Burial-grounds not laid out as Open Places for the Public Use

Note (1). although most of them are neatly kept, a few are used as store-yards, etc. and others are open at times.

Note (2) churches described as 'burned' were those destroyed in the Great Fire of London in 1666 (see Appendix D).

288. **The Temple Churchyard**: Partly public thoroughfare, partly closed.

The Churchyards of:
289. **St Andrew, Holborn**.
290. **Christ Church, Newgate Street**, on the site of the western end of the church of the Greyfriars.
291. **St Ann, Blackfriars**: Two grounds; the western end is the site of the burned church.
292. **St Andrews by the Wardrobe, Queen Victoria Street:** very little left.
293. **St Bartholomew the Great**: On the site of the ancient nave, the 'Green- ground' on the site of the south transept, and a remnant of the 'Poor-ground' on the north side.
294. **St Dionys Backchurch, Lime Street**.
295. **St Bartholomew the Less – in the hospital**: At one time it extended further south.
296. **St Giles, Cripplegate, with the 'Green-ground', an extension to the south**: Often open, neatly kept.
297. **St Alphege, London Wall**: The churchyard does not adjoin the church. It contains a portion of the old wall.
298. **St Ann and St Agnes, Gresham Street**.

St. Mildred's, Bread Street, about 1825

299. **St John Zachary, Gresham Street : Site of burned church**.

300. **St Mary Staining, Oat Lane**: Site of burned church.

301. **St Alban's, Wood Street**.

302. **St Peter Cheap, Wood Street**: Site of burned church.

303. **St Vedast, Foster Lane**.

304. **St Mildred, Bread Street**: Yard full of ladders.

305. **St Mary Somerset, Thames Street**: Store-yard for old iron, behind the tower. Most of this ground has gone.

306. **St Peter, Paul's Wharf**: Site of burned church.

307. **St Martin Vintry, Queen Street**: No church.

St. Peter's, Cornhill, 1817

308. **St Thomas the Apostle, Queen Street**: Little left except a large vault.

309. **St Mary Aldermary, Watling Street**.

310. **St Antholin, Watling Street**: Very little left except one great vault.

311. **St Pancras, Pancras Lane**: Site of burned church.

312. **St Benet Sherehog, Pancras Lane**: Site of burned church.

313. **St Martin Pomeroy (St Olave's Jewry), Ironmonger Lane, the site of St Martin's Church, used as St Olave's Churchyard when that became a private garden**.

314. **St Stephen, Coleman Street**.

315. **St Mildred, Poultry**: given by Thomas Morsted in 1420. Almost lost in 1594. Abridged before 1633 and enlarged in 1693.

316. **St Matthew, Friday Street**.

317. **St John, Watling Street**: Site of burned church.

318. **St Michael, Queenhithe**: Private garden for St James's Rectory.

319. **St Martin, Ludgate – Stationers' Hall Court**: The vaults are under its ground.

320. **St Christopher le Stocks**: Garden of the Bank of England since 1780.

321. **St Michael, Cornhill**: Some shops were built in this ground in 1690.

322. **St Peter, Cornhill**.

323. **St Stephen, Walbrook**: Encroached upon in 1693.

324. **St Margaret, Lothbury**: Improved and planted at the expense of Dr. Edwin Freshfield F.S.A,

325. **St Martin Outwich, Camomile Street**: The burial-ground of the Priory of St Augustine Papey; given by Robert Hyde in 1538.

326. **St Michael Paternoster Royal, College Hill**.

327. **St James, Garlickhithe**.

328. **St Nicholas Cole Abbey, Queen Victoria Street**: Very little left.

329. **St Swithin, Cannon Street**: Additional ground; one adjoining the church has gone.

330. **St Allhallows the Great, Upper Thames Street**.

331. **Allhallows the Less, Upper Thames Street**: Site of burned church.

332. **St Laurence Pountney, Cannon Street**: Two grounds, one being the site of the burned church.

333. **St Martin Orgar, Cannon Street**: Site of burned church.

Allhallows', Staining, 1838

334. **St George, Botolph Lane**.

335. **St Mary at Hill, Eastcheap**: Saved by the City Church and Churchyard Protection Society in 1879.

336. **St Andrew Undershaft, Leadenhall Street**.

337. **St Catherine Cree, Leadenhall Street**: A part of the cemetery of the Holy Trinity Priory, Aldgate.

338. **St Helen's, Bishopgate**: This is very often open, but not provided with seats.

339. **St Ethelburga, Bishopsgate**.

340. **St Clement, Eastcheap**.

341. **St Leonard, Fish Street Hill**: Site of burned church.

342. **St Magnus the Martyr, London Bridge**.

343. **St Mary Woolnoth, Lombard Street**: In danger at the present time.

344. **St Nicholas Acons, Lombard Street**.

345. **St Edmund King and Martyr, Lombard Street**: The property of the Salters' Company. Laid out as a garden with seats.

346. **Allhallows, Lombard Street**: Closed in the cholera year, 1849.

347. **St Gabriel, Fenchurch Street**: The gift of Helming Legget.

348. **St Allhallows, Staining, Mark Lane**: Church destroyed in 1870 except the tower. The property of the Clothworkers' Company.

349. **St Olave's, Hart Street**.

350. **Allhallows, Barking, Tower Hill**.

351. **St Dunstan's in the East, Lower Thames Street**: Its opening is under consideration.

352. **The Burial-ground of Christ's Hospital**: This has been almost covered with buildings, but a small piece of it remains as a yard near the great hall.

353. **The Burial-ground of the Greyfriars**: This is a courtyard, surrounded by cloisters, in Christ's Hospital, used as a playground by the boys.

354. **St James's Churchyard, Duke Street**: This is used as a playground by the Aldgate Ward Schools.

355. **Additional ground for St Bride's, Fleet Street**: This is off Farringdon Street; it is about 750 square yards in extent, and is used as a volunteer drill-ground. There are no tombstones, and the ground is untidy. Given by the Earl of Dorset.

356. **St Mary's Roman Catholic Church ground, Finsbury Square**: Very little left.

357. **Bridewell Burial-ground**: This is about 900 square yards in size, and is at the corner of Tudor

and Dorset Streets. It was the burial ground of the hospital, which has been removed. It is now a very untidy yard, boarded up with a rough advertisement hoarding, in the occupation of H.S. Foster, builder, of No. 7 Tudor Street. It would make a good public playground.

Burial-grounds which have been paved and added to the public footpath but are still traceable; these are the churchyards of:

358. **St Mary, Abchurch Lane**: This was part of the pavement about 160 years ago, with posts round it.

359. **St Margaret Pattens, Rood Lane**.

360. **St Laurence Jewry, by the Guildhall**.

361. **St Michael Bassishaw, Basinghall Street**: Two good trees.

362. **St Benet Fink, Threadneedle Street**: Railed in, with the statue of George Peabody, banker and philanthropist, in it.

363. **The Cloisters of the Augustine Friars**: Lately discovered on the north side of the Dutch Church, Austin Friars Square forming part of the site.

Burial Ground still in Use

364. **Newgate Burial-ground**: A passage used for the interment of those who are executed; 10 feet wide and 85 feet in length (see Appendix D).

APPENDIX B

Burial Grounds which have been entirely demolished and replaced by New Streets, Railway-lines and Stations, Public Buildings, Office Blocks and Private Houses

Some of the following replacements reported by Mrs Holmes have themselves been later replaced – by your house or office?

The City

There were Roman Cemeteries in various parts of the City. Sepulchral remains have been found in:

1. Newgate Street.
2. Ludgate.
3. Camomile Street.
4. St Mary at Hill.
5. St Dunstan's in the East.
6. St Paul's Churchyard.
7. Bishopsgate Churchyard.

St. Dunstan's-in-the-East

Name of Churchyard or Burial Ground, and what occupies the Site

8. **Burial grounds of St Martin le Grand and St Leonard, Foster Lane**: Now the General Post Office.

9. **Jews' original Burial-ground**: Now Jewin Street and neighbourhood.

10. **St Nicholas Shambles**: Now Newgate street.

11. **St Benet's, Paul's Wharf.**

Now merged into St Benet's Hill

12. **The Workhouse Ground, Shoe Lane, belonging to St Andrew's, Holborn**: Then the Farringdon Market occupied the site, and a street has now taken its place, called Farringdon Avenue

The Churchyard of St. Benet, Paul's Wharf, 1838

13. **Allhallows, Honey Lane**: The Old City of London School was built on its site.

14. **St Mary le Bow**: Then was called Bow Church-yard, now warehouses and streets full of vans.

15. **St John's, Cloak Lane**: Now taken by the District Railway in 1879 for Cannon Street Station.

16. **St Mary Bothaw**: Now Cannon Street Station, South-Eastern Railway.

17. **St Mary Mounthaw**: Now taken for Queen Victoria Street.

18. **St Nicholas Olave**: Now taken for Queen Victoria Street.

19. **St Mary Magdalen**: Now taken for Queen Victoria Street.

20. **Elsing Spital Priory**: Now warehouses, London Wall.

21. **St Peter le Poer, Broad Street**: Now houses in Broad Street.

22. **St Thomas Acons**: Now Mercers' Hall.

23. **St Bartholomew's Priory, Smithfield**: This had a cemetery attached, which is now covered by the buildings near the south transept of the church.

24. **St Bartholomew's Hospital**: Now the West Wing of the Hospital Burial-ground.

25. **St Swithin, Cannon Street**: Now roadway on north side of church.

26. **St Dunstan in the West, Fleet Street**: Now probably the north end of the church.

27. **St Michael le Querne**: Now Cheapside

28. **Additional ground to Christ Church, Moorgate Street**: Now southern end of St Bartholomew's Hospital.

29. **St Mary Colechurch**: Now Old Jewry.

30. **St Margaret Moses, Friday Street**: Now Cannon Street.

31. **Garden in Hosier Lane, Friday Street**: built upon about 1560.

32. **Holy Trinity the Less, Trinity Lane**: Now Mansion House Station.

33. **St Mary Axe, Leadenhall Street**: Now houses on west side of the street called St Mary Axe.

34. **St Mary Woolchurch Haw**: Now the Mansion House.

35. **St Bartholomew by the Exchange**: Now Threadneedle Street.

36. **Bethlem Burial-ground (also called Rowe's)**: Now Liverpool Street Station.

37. **St Benet, Gracechurch Street**: Now corner of Fenchurch Street.

38. **St Margaret's, New Fish Street**: Now the Metropolitan Railway.

39. **St Andrew Hubbard**: Now houses between Botolph Lane and Love Lane. The old King's Weigh House Chapel was on this site.

40. **St Botolph's, Billingsgate (Lower Ground)**: Now warehouse in Lower Thames Street, with terra cotta heads on the frontage.

41. **Garden of Hundsdon House, Blackfriars (French Embassy)**: Ninety-five corpses buried here in 1623 after an accident.Site now disappeared.

42. **Pest Field, Hand Alley**: Now New Street, Bishopsgate Street.

43. **The Churchyard of the Dutch Church, Austin Friars**: This Burial Ground was on the south side of the Dutch Church, now built over.

44. **St Michael, Crooked Lane**: Now King William Street.

45. **St James' Hermitage Burial-ground**: Now houses south of the postern and the south wall of St Giles Church-yard, Cripplegate.

46. **Cemetery of the Crutched Friars**: Now south of Fenchurch Street.

St Marylebone

47. **Churchyard of Old Tyburn Church at Tyburn**: Now Marylebone Court House, Stratford Place.

48. **Burial place for those executed at Tyburn**: Now corner of Upper Bryanston Street and Edgeware Road (see Appendix D).

49. **Pest Fields, Craven Hill, probaby never used**: Now Craven Hill Gardens.

Hammersmith

50. **Convent Burial-ground, King Street**: Now part of the buildings of the Convent of the Sacred Heart, rebuilt by Cardinal Manning.

St Margaret and St John, Westminster

51. **Buckingham Chapel, Palace Street**: Now brewery on the south side.

St Martin's in the Fields

52. **St Martin's additional ground**: Now part of the building of the National Gallery.

53. **Burial-ground for the Friends of the Westminster division**: Now Castle Street, Long Acre.

54. **Burial-ground of the St Mary Rounceval Convent**: Now Northumberland Avenue.

St James's, Westminster

55. **Pest Field**: Now Golden Square and district around it.

The Strand

56. **Additional ground for St Martin's in the Fields**: Then French Chapel, Crown Street, Soho, later Charing Cross Road.

57. **German Burial-ground, Savoy**: Now Medical Examination Hall and Savoy Chambers.

58. **Old Somerset House Cemetery**: Now Somerset House.

59. **Westminster Convent Burial-ground**: Now part of Covent Garden Market.

60. **Almshouse Ground, Clements Lane**: Now the New Law Courts.

61 **Burial-ground by the Workhouse, St Paul's, Covent Garden**: Now possibly the Floral Arcade.

62. **Cemetery of old St Mary le Strand**: Now Somerset House, etc.

St Giles' in the Fields

63. **The Workhouse Burial-ground**: Now part of the Workhouse in Shorts Gardens.

Holborn

64. **St Sepulchre's Additional Ground, Durham Yard**: Now Great Northern Goods Dep't.

65. **St Sepulchre's Workhouse Ground, Durham Yard**: Now as above. This was the larger of the two.

66. **Pardon Churchyard, Charter-house**: Then Wilderness Row, subsequently Clerkenwell Road.

67. **Baptist Chapel Ground, Glasshouse Yard**: Now Goswell Road, just to the south of St Thomas's, Charterhouse.

Clerkenwell

68. **Nuns' Burial-ground**: Now the houses on the west side of St James' Walk.

69. **St James's Additional Ground, Ray Street**: Now Farringdon Road and the Railway.

70. **Corporation Row Burial-pit**: Now workmen's dwellings on the north side of Corporation Street.

71. **Priory Cemetery**: Now St John's Square, etc.

72. **St Thomas', Golden Lane**: Now factory on the west side of St Mary's Church, Charterhouse, Playhouse Yard.

73. **Pest Field, Old Street**: Now Beth Street and many acres to the north.

74. **Pest Field, Mount Mill**: Now Seward Street, Goswell Road, north side.

75. **Cupid's Court Ground, Golden Lane**: Now Offices etc., to the north of Brackley Street.

Shoreditch

76. **Gloucester Street Chapel Ground**: Now Gas, Light and Coke Company's premises.

77. **Shoreditch Burial-ground, Hoxton**: Now wing of the Workhouse which was built in 1884.

78. **Burial-ground by the Gold-Smith's Almshouses**: Now new block of workmen's dwellings on the west side of Goldsmith Row.
79. **Worship Street Baptist Chapel Ground**: Now London and North Western Railway Dep't.

Stoke Newington

80. **Abney Congregational Chapel, Church Street**: Now school buildings.

Bethnal Green

81. **Roman Catholic Ground**: Now Cambridge Road.
82. **Pest Field belonging to Stepney**: Now land south of Lisbon Street and Collingwood Street.

Whitechapel

83. **Roman Cemetery**: Now Goodman's Fields.
84. **Burial-ground, Whitechapel Road**: Now Whitechapel Workhouse.
85. **St Katherine's, near to the Tower of London**: Now St Katherine's Docks.
86. **Additional Ground to St Katherine's**: Now St Katherine Docks.
87. **Bone Yard, Gower's Walk**: Now houses.
88. **Zoar Chapel, Alie Street**: Now warehouses, shops and a forge.
89. **Pest Field, Spital Square**: Now St Mary's Church, etc.
90. **Pest Field east of the Royal Mint and Cemetery of the Convent of St Mary of Grace**: Now the Royal Mint.
91. **Pest Field, Petticoat Lane**: Now built over with houses, etc.
92. **Tower of London Burial-ground outside the moat wall**: Now demolished for Tower Bridge.

93. **St Mary Spital Priory**: Now Spital Square and district.

94. **Pest Field or Plague Pit in Gower's Walk**: Now Messrs. Kinloch's new buildings.

95. **Mill Yard Sabbatarian Chapel**: Now the Railway by Leman Street Station.

96. **German Church, Hooper Street**: Now the Railway.

Limehouse

97. **Roman Cemetery**: Now Sun Tavern Fields, Shadwell.

98. **Friends' Burial-ground**: Now Wapping Street.

Mile End Old Town

99. **Rose Lane Chapel Ground** : Now East London Railway, public house and shops close to Stepney Station.

St George the Martyr, Southwark

100. **London Road Chapel Ground**: Now tailor's shop on the east side of London Road.

101. **Baptist Chapel Ground, Sheer's Alley**: Now Wilmott's Buildings.

102. **Zion Chapel, Borough**: Now workmen's dwellings, Chapel Court.

103. **Friends' Burial-ground, Worcester Street**: Now London Bridge and Charing Cross Railway.

104. **Chapel Burial-ground, Ewer Street**: Now London Bridge and Charing Cross Railway.

105. **Baptist Chapel Ground, Pepper Street (Duke Street Park)**: Now houses at the corner of Pepper Street.

106. **St Margaret's Southwark**: Now Borough High Street and Market.

St Olave's

107. **Additional Ground, St Olave's**: Now St Thomas Street.

108. **Flemish Burial-ground, Carter Lane**: Now approach to London Bridge Railway Station.

109. **Mazepond Baptist Chapel**: Now Guy's Hospital Medical School.

110. **Baptist Chapel, Dipping Alley**: Now Fair Street or Charles Street, Horselydown.

Bermondsey

111. **Roman Cemetery**: Now Snow Fields, Union Street, and Deverell Street (Newington).

Greenwich

112. **Roman Cemetery**: Now neighbourhood of Blackheath.

Woolwich

113. **Bethlem Chapel Ground, Charles Street**: Now Club House.

APPENDIX C

Churches and Chapels with Vaults under them that have been used for Interments but with no Graveyards attached

A re these ecclesiastical buildings still standing – or could there be, unbeknownst to you, a coffin-filled 'cellar' under your house?

The Foundling Chapel, W.C.
Lincoln Inn's Chapel and Cloisters, W.C.
Gray's Inn Chapel, W.C.
Ely Place Chapel, E.C.
Lambeth Palace Chapel, S.E.
St Pancras New Church, W.C.
Camden Chapel, St Pancras, N.W.
Christ Church, Marylebone, N.W.
Holy Trinity, Marylebone, N.W.
Holy Trinity, Islington, N.
St John's, Upper Holloway, N.
St John's, Paddington, W.
St Barnabas, Kensington, W.
All Saints, Islington, N.
Aske's Hospital Chapel, Hoxton, N.
St Barnabas, King's Square, E.C.
St Thomas', Charterhouse, E.C.

St Marks, Clerkenwell, E.C.
St Mark's, North Audley Street, W.
Grosvenor Chapel, South Audley Street, W.
Hanover Chapel, Regent Street, W. (about to be demolished).
St Peter's, Pimlico, S.W.
St Stephen's, Westminster, S.W.
St James's, Clapham, S.W.
St Anne's, Wandsworth, S.W.
Holy Trinity, Newington, S.E.
St Mary Magdalen's, Peckham, S.E.
Holy Trinity, Little Queen Street, W.C.
Weslyan Chapel, Great Queen Street, W.C.
Mission Chapel, Little Wyld Street, W.C.
Elim Street, Fetter Lane, E.C.
Baptist Church, Blandford Street, N.W.
Roman Catholic Chapel, Grove Road, N.W.
Congregational Chapel, Kentish Town, N.W.
Brunswick Chapel, Nile End Road, E. (now connected with Charrington's Assembly Hall).
Baptist Chapel, Romney Street, S.W.
Surrey Chapel, Blackfriars Road, S.E. (now a machine manufactory)
Queen Street Chapel, Woolwich, S.E.

Note: Some vaults, such as those under the Guildhall Chapel, the Rolls Chapel, and the notorious Enon Chapel, Clements Lane, have disappeared with the building; and it must be remembered that the City churches that have lost their churchyards, have vaults underneath them, and so have other buildings, such as the Charterhouse Chapel and cloisters, the burial-grounds there being of much later date and detached from the church.

APPENDIX D

SUPPLEMENT
OF NOTES TO
CHAPTERS

Foreword
The Plagues which ravaged London:
These appalling scourges are frequently referred to
throughout by Mrs Holmes. They occurred in an age
when there was no innoculation, no immunisation,
no proper medicine – indeed no one even knew what
caused them! In these days, when the merest possibility
of a flu epidemic causes some apprehension, it is hard to
visualise the scenes of the utmost nightmarish proportions
which took place whenever the plague was at its height in
London, and who better to describe the appalling effects
than one who witnessed an outbreak at first-hand and
who described all its horrors so graphically, but the author
and journalist Daniel Defoe (d.1731);

'I went all the first Part of the Time freely about the
streets, tho' not so freely as to run my self into apparent
Danger, except when they dug the great Pit in the Churchyard of our Parish of Aldgate; a terrible Pit it was, and I
could not resist my Curiosity to go and see it; as near as
I may judge, it was about 40 Foot in length and about
15 or 16 Foot deep; and at the time I first looked at it,
about nine Foot deep; but it was said they dug it near
twenty Foot deep afterwards, in one part of it, till they
could go no deeper for the Water; for they had, it seems,
dug several large Pits before this, for the Plague was long

a-coming to our Parish, yet when it did come, there was
no Parish in or about London where it raged with such
Violence as in the two Parishes of Aldgate and White-
Chapel.

I got admission into the Church-Yard by being
acquainted with one Sexton who attended, who tho' he
did not refuse me at all, yet earnestly persuaded me not to
go, telling me very seriously, for he was a good, religious
and sensible man, that it was indeed their Business and
Duty to venture and to run all Hazards (take all risks); and
that in it they might hope to be preserved; but that I had no
apparent Call to it, by my own Curiosity, which, he said,
he believed I would not pretend, was sufficient to justify
my running that Hazard. I told him I had been pressed in
my Mind to go, and that it might be an instructing Sight,
that might not be without its Uses. Nay, said the good
man, you will venture upon that Score; Name of God, go
in, for depend on it, 'twill be a Sermon to you, it may be
the best that you ever heard in all your life. 'Tis a speaking
sight, said he, and has a Voice with it, and a loud one, to
call us to Repentance; and with that he opened the Door
and said, Go, if you will.

His Discourse had shock'd my Resolution a little, and
I stood wavering for a good while, but just at that interval
I saw two Links (men bearing torches to light the way)
come over from the End of the Minories, and heard the
Bell-man, and then appeared a Dead-Cart, as they call
it, coming along the Streets, so I could no longer resist
my Desire to see it, and went in. There was no Body, as
I could perceive at first, in the Church-Yard, or on going
into it, but the Buryers and the Fellow that drove the Cart,
or rather led the Horse and Cart, but when they came up
towards the Pit, they saw a Man muffled up in a brown
Cloak and making Motions with his Hands, under his
Cloak, as if he was in a great Agony, and the Buryers
immediately gathered about him, supposing he was
one of those poor delirious or desperate Creatures that
used to pretend, as I have said, to bury themselves; he
said nothing as he walked about, but two or three times

groaned very deeply, and loud, and sighed as if he would break his Heart.

When the Buryers came up to him they soon found that he was one opressed with a dreadful Weight of Grief indeed, having had his Wife and several of his Children, all in that Cart, that was just come in with him, and he followed in an Agony and excess of Sorrow. He mourned heartedly, as was easy to see, but with a kind of Masculine Grief that could not give itself Vent by Tears, and calmly desired the Buryers to let him alone, saying he would only see the Bodies thrown in and then go away, so they left off importuning him, but no sooner had the Cart turned round, and the Bodies shot into the Pit promiscuously (casually), which was a Surprize to him, for he at least expected they would have been decently laid in, tho' he was afterwards convinced that was impracticable; I say, no sooner did he see the Sight, but he cry'd out aloud, unable to contain himself; I could not hear what he said, but he went backwards two or three steps and fell down in a Swoon. The Buryers ran to him and took him up and in a little while he came to himself and they led him away to the Pye-Tavern over against the End of Houndsditch, where they took care of him. He look'd into the Pit again, as he went away, but the Buryers had covered the Bodies so immediately with throwing in Earth, that tho' there was Light enough, for there were Lanthorns and Candles in them, placed all night round the sides of the Pit upon the Heaps of Earth, seven or eight, or perhaps more, yet nothing more of the Bodies could be seen.

This was a Mournful Scene indeed, and affected me almost as much as the rest; but what happened next was awful and full of Terror; the Cart had in it sixteen or seventeen Bodies in it, some were wrapped up in Linen Sheets, some in Rugs, some little other than naked, or so Loose that what Covering they had, fell from them in the shooting out of the Cart, and they fell quite naked among the Rest; but the Matter was not much to them, or the Indecency to any one else, seeing they were all dead and were to be huddled together in the common

Grave of Mankind, as we may call it, for here was no Difference made, but Poor and Rich went together; there was no other way of Burials, neither was it possible there should, for Coffins were not to be had, for the prodigious Numbers that fell in such a Calamity as this.

It was reported by way of Scandal upon the Buryers, that if any Corpses was delivered to them, decently wrap't up, as we called it then, in a Winding Sheet ty'd over the Head and Feet, which some did, and which was generally of good Linen, I say, it was reported that the Buryers were so wicked as to strip Them in the Cart, and carry them quite Naked to the Pit; but as I cannot easily credit any thing so vile among Christians, and at a time so filled with Terror, as that was, I can only relate it and leave it undetermined.'

And these few victims of the Plague were but a few of the many tens of thousands whose corpses now lie mouldering beneath today's play-grounds, streets and housing estates.

Chapter 2 – The Graveyards of Priories and Convents

'Four heads found in Pots';
As included in my *Who's Who of British Beheadings/ Severed Heads* published Andre Deutsch 2000/2003, an excerpt of John Stow's *Survey of London* related how:

'They came to an old wall of great thickness, where appeared a kind of cupboard. Which, being opened, they found four Pots or Cases of fine pewter, thick, with covers of the same, and rings fastened to the top to take up (lift) or put down at pleasure. The Cases were flat before and rounded behind, and in each of them was reposited a human head, inconsumed by the Fire, preserved, as it seems, by Art; with the Teeth and Hair, the Flesh of a tawny colour, wrapt up in black silk, almost consumed. And a certain Substance, of a blackish colour, crumbled into dust, lying at the bottom of the Pots.

One of these Pots, with the head in it, I saw in October 1703, being in the custody of Mr Prestbury, then Sope

Maker in Smithfield. The Pot was inscribed on the inside of the Cover in a scrawling Character – which might be used in the time of Henry VIII – 'J. Cornelius'. This Head was without any neck, having short red hair upon it, thick, and it could not be pulled off; and yellow hair upon the temples, a little bald on top, perhaps a Tonsure, the forepart of the Nose sunk, the Mouth gaping, ten sound teeth, others had been plucked out; the skin like tanned leather, the Features of the Face visible. There was one body near it, buried, and without its head, but no other bodies found. The three other heads had some of the necks joined to them, and had broader and plainer Razure (pattern of head-shaving), which showed them to be priests. These three are now dispersed. One was given to an Apothecary, another entrusted with a Parish Clerk who, it is thought, got money by the shewing of it. It is probable that they were at last privately procured and conveyed abroad and now become Holy Relicks. Who these were, there is no Record as I know of, nor had any of them any Names inscribed but one. To me they seem to have been zealous priests or friars executed for Treason, whereof there were many in the Rebellion in Lincolnshire in 1580, or others who had denied the King's Supremacy, and here deposited by these Black Friars.'

Research by the historian Dr Challoner into the head contained in the pot bearing a name confirmed this to be more or less correct. John Cornelius, or Mohun, was born in 1557 in Bodmin, of Irish parents. After studying at Oxford, he went to Rheims and from thence to Rome, where he studied to become a Roman Catholic priest. Dedicated and devoted to his cause, he returned to England in 1583, to travel the country bringing spiritual guidance and comfort to the persecuted Catholics during the reign of Queen Elizabeth. Constantly hunted by the authorities, he, like his brother priests, had to be prepared to conceal himself at a moment's notice in priest-holes (secret hiding places ingeniously constructed in country houses, behind panelling, under stairways, even beneath fire-places) for days on end, without food or water. Cramped and confined in little more than small cupboards, not daring to make a sound, they can only be admired for their endurance.

The official searchers, known as pursuivants, were cunning and expert; counting windows from outside a house, then again from inside, might reveal a hidden room; measuring adjoining rooms could disclose hidden cavities; panelling would be tapped to identify hollow spaces behind. Should all these measures fail, the pursuivants would loudly discuss their disappointment and intended departure, only to creep back and, impersonating the house servants, tap on the walls and joyfully announce to the fugitives that the coast was clear, that they could now come out, stretch their limbs, eat and drink. Then they would pounce as their wretched, starving and thirsty victims emerged from their cramped hiding places.

In April 1594 John Cornelius visited the widow of Sir John Arundel for the purpose of celebrating Mass. While engaged in his administrations, a servant, either for reward or in obedience of the law, reported the priest's presence to the pursuivants, and on their approach, the priest hastily sought refuge in one of the many hiding places. While some of the searchers made much commotion in one part of the house, shouting and knocking loudly on walls, others waited elsewhere, quietly listening as the hours dragged by. And on hearing a muffled cough, they broke down the panelling and arrested the fugitive priest.

As Cornelius was being led away, a relative of the family, Mr Bosgrave, seeing that the captive was bare-headed, put his own hat on the priest's head, a charitable action which immediately resulted in his own arrest. Two of the house servants, Terence Carey and Patrick Salmon were also taken into custody for failing to report the presence of the priest themselves.

John Cornelius was taken to London and there racked in an attempt to persuade him to reveal the whereabouts of other priests. On his refusal he was tried and found guilty of high treason. At Dorchester on 2 July 1594, Mr Bosgrave, Carey and Salmon were hanged; Cornelius was hanged, drawn and quartered. It was reported that his head was used as a football by the bigoted mob before being displayed over the city gates, where it remained for some time until removed after protests by the townsfolk.

By devious means the head was then procured by fellow Catholics, who presented it to the Black Friars in London as a holy relic. There, stored in the crypt with those of other martyrs, it was revered until, more than seventy years later, the Great Fire reduced the buildings to rubble, leaving the caskets unscathed underground.

The Royal Mint
Established in the Tower of London in the late thirteenth century, by 1552 it was the only mint in the country and had been, indeed, the only one authorised to manufacture gold coinage, a machine being used to slice the long bars of precious metal into the thin slivers for the actual coins. Queen Elizabeth visited in 1561, and following the *Act of Union* with Scotland in 1707, the new currency which was then required, was produced under the watchful eye of the Master of the Mint, Sir Isaac Newton. In 1744 thirty-two wagon-loads of Spanish bullion, the cargo of a Spanish galleon captured by Commodore Anson in the Pacific, was off-loaded on Tower Wharf and transported into the Mint, there to be made into English gold coins, no doubt gladdening the heart of the then Chancellor of the Exchequer! But the Royal Mint needed to expand and so in 1810 it moved into new buildings immediately north-east of the Tower, vacating them again in more recent years, the buildings being converted into private apartments, although the imposing façade remained in place. One wonders whether the residents are aware that, as mentioned in the text, prior to there being the Royal Mint on that site, there stood the Cistercian Abbey of Our Lady of Grace, or of St Mary of Grace, later becoming known, in contradistinction to Westminster Abbey, as

Eastminster Abbey! As stated by Mrs Holmes, it was built on land first acquired by John Corey in 1348 and used as a plague pit in which to bury victims of the Black Death. The Abbey itself existed until 1539, the building being valued at £546, and subsequently became occupied by a naval store and bakehouse for ships' biscuits.

Katharine's Convent
This was first known as St Katharine's Hospital and was founded in 1148 by Queen Matilda (1103-1152), immediately east of the Tower of London. It maintained a close connection with the queens of England, who were its patrons, and was intended to support thirteen poor persons; among its staff were priests whose religious duties included saying Mass for the souls of Baldwin and Matilda, the royal children. St Katharine's was given the wardenship of London Bridge in 1264 but had to forfeit some of its land to the Tower authorities in Edward I's reign. The Hospital was reorganised by Edward III's consort Philippa of Hainault (1314-1369) who, believing that red or green clothing was a sign of dissolute living, insisted that the inmates wore straight coats bearing the Wheel symbol of St Katharine. In 1343 a new church was built and in the following century a fair lasting twenty-one days was held annually on St James' Day, 25 July, on Tower Hill.

In 1796 Parliament passed an Act which would clear the site of all buildings, religious and otherwise, to allow for an extension to St Katharine's Dock, and work eventually started in 1827, necessitating the demolition of 1,250 houses and shops, taverns and tenements; 11,300 residents had to seek accommodation elsewhere. When completed, the second vessel to enter the new dock was the Russian ship *Mary*, which 'exhibited on board the pleasing spectacle of forty veteran pensioners from Greenwich, all of whom had served under Admiral Lord Nelson at the Battle of Trafalgar.' It was at this wharf that steamboat passengers from the Continent generally landed, but by the end of the twentieth century the cavernous warehouses, in which more than a hundred thousand tons of goods off-loaded from the merchant shipping could be stored, had been converted into private and expensive residences, a shopping centre and large hotel also occupying the site; St Katharine's Dock itself is now a harbour for luxurious yachts and powered sea-going craft.

Chapter 3 – St Paul's, The Tower and the City Churchyards
Tower of London Churchyards

1. The Chapel Royal of St Peter ad Vincula, St Peter in Chains, stands in the north-west corner of the inner ward. It was built during the reign of Edward 1 (1272-1307), adjoining the site of an earlier chapel, the bill for clearing the area amounting to forty-six shillings and eight pence, and beneath its floor lie the remains of the three decapitated Queens of England, and other unfortunate victims of the sovereigns of the day, who died beneath the axe on Tower Hill.

To the millions of tourists who visit the Tower each year, Tower Green is simply the neat lawns fronting the Chapel, and are not aware that the grass, and the ground now covered by part of the Waterloo Block and the Jewel House, cover the site of the ancient graveyard in which, together with those of countless others, reportedly were buried the remains of three men whose involvement with a queen of England brought about, not only their own, horrific deaths, but the beheadings of the woman herself – Queen Anne Boleyn.

Henry Norris, Usher of the Black Rod, Gentleman of the Privy Chamber, and Sir Francis Weston, Knight Companion of the Bath, were two members of the small group of courtiers with whom Queen Anne surrounded herself in order to relieve the boredom of Palace life. Among the courtiers was a spinet-player,

Mark Smeton, who entertained the company by playing his music. However Henry VIII's right-hand man Thomas Cromwell, who was markedly hostile to Anne, suspected that rather more than singing roundelays and tripping the light fantastic took place during such get-togethers, and by administering a little gentle persuasion by means of the rack, extracted a confession, true or false, from Smeton, and passed the information on to his master. On the following day, while attending a tournament at Greenwich, Anne dropped a handkerchief and Norris picked it up and returned it to her; on seeing that, Henry abruptly left the gathering, and shortly afterwards Smeton, Norris and Weston found themselves in the Tower. Charged with adulterous association with the Queen, all were put on trial and found guilty. Weston and Norris, being Gentlemen of the Court, were given the privilege of execution by the chivalrous method of cold steel, the axe, and so, on 17 May 1536, they were decapitated in front of the crowds of Londoners who had congregated around the scaffold on Tower Hill. Norris's severed head was claimed by his relatives and was interred in the private chapel of their manor house at Ockwells near Maidenhead. His body, and that of Weston, according to Wriothesley's *Chronicles* were 'buried within the Tower in the churchyeard of the same in one grave.' Two days later, on 19 May, the Queen herself was beheaded only yards away from their grave, her remains then buried before the Chapel altar. Despite Smeton having been promised, while being racked, that if he confessed, he would be pardoned, he quickly found out that Tudor promises didn't really mean what they said, and he was not only decapitated but quartered as well.

2. Bodies of those aristocrats decapitated outside on Tower Hill were buried 'under the floor' of St Peter's Chapel until they were exhumed during Queen Victoria's reign and decently reinterred in large chests

which were then walled up in the Crypt, but other bodies remain under the paving stones at its entrance, the remains of three Scottish soldiers who were shot by firing squad within the Tower. In the Spring of 1743 Lord Semple's Regiment, which later became the Black Watch, was based north of the Border and were ordered to march to London, there to be inspected by George II. By 3 April, exhausted and foot-sore, they camped on Finchley Common, and then disturbing rumours began to circulate that they had been tricked and were instead destined to be shipped to the colonies in America and the West Indies. Far being ordinary soldiers, these were mainly the sons of gentlemen farmers with families, homesteads and small estates to look after, who even bought the weapons with which they were expected to fight. Discontent grew, especially when, on 17 May, they were informed that the regiment was actually to be shipped to Flanders and from thence to the battlefront. At that, although some soldiers accepted the situation under protest, more than a hundred of them set out to march back to Scotland, accompanied, if not encouraged by, Corporals Samuel McPherson and Malcolm McPherson, their spirits bouyed up by the tunes played by Piper Donal McDonnal. The authorities immediately swung into action, the *London Gazette* stating that the Lords Justice had put a bounty on them, offering a reward of forty shillings for each man captured; three companies of dragoons were also sent in pursuit, eventually catching up with the deserters at Lady Wood, Northampton. No resistance was offered, and all were escorted back to London. During their march north, eight had been taken ill or had died, one of the latter reportedly being buried in Lady Wood at a spot traditionally known as the 'Soldiers' Grave.'

Back in London they were imprisoned in the Tower, being allowed 'a pd. and a half of bread, half a pd. of good chees and a Pynt of Oatmeal Porrige p. day, and

4d. p. day for each man.' At their Courts Martial, the two corporals and a Private Farquar Shaw, who had threatened to strike an officer when ordered to return to duty, were charged with being ringleaders and, being found guilty, were sentenced to death, the rest sentenced to be sent to the colonies. It was reported that when the yeoman warder went to tell Samuel McPherson the Court's finding 'he carried with him two Centinels for fear any Accident may befall; Samuel started with Surprize and asked with some emotion "How must I die?". The Warder replied "You are to be Shot, sir." Samuel then asked if he might be allowed Pen and Ink, and when the post went for Scotland? The Warder told him the Night, but that he could not live to receive any return.'

The executions took place in the Tower on 18 July 1743, the condemned men – wearing their shrouds under their uniforms and with their caps pulled down over their eyes – kneeling on planks, their backs to the wall of St Peter's Chapel. Their comrades had been formed up in a semi-circle facing the doomed trio and guarded by an outer semi-circle of the 3rd Regiment of Guards (ironically lately becoming the Scots Guards), many of whom were visibly upset at having to witness the execution of fellow Scottish soldiers.

The firing squad, consisted of eighteen soldiers, four to aim at each man, with six in reserve, was under the command of Sergeant-Major Ellison. As much mercy as possible was shown, it being reported that 'the firing squad advanced on their Tiptoes so to make the least noise, their Pieces (muskets) ready cocked for fear of the Click disturbing the Prisoners, and were, by the Wave of a Handkerchief, without any Word of Command, directed to "Make ready – Present – Fire", which they did, all at once, and the three men fell at the Same moment dead, but as Shaw and Samuel McFarson, had some little tremors and convulsions, the men of the Reserve had to shoot them through the head.'

Their corpses were immediately put into coffins, the Lieutenant of the Tower, General Williamson, stating afterwards 'There was not much blood spilt, but what there was, I ordered it immediately to be covered with earth and their grave to be Leveld so that no remains of their execution might be perceived.' Now their monument is just plain, unmarked grey paving stone, stepped on by the tens of thousands of visitors who enter the Royal Chapel each year.

Considerably more people than that number must have also walked over another set of human remains which were discovered while excavations were taking place near the Lanthorn Tower in 1976. Seen by the author, the complete skeleton lay about five metres below the surface of the surrounding earth, huddled on its back, with knees drawn up, indicating that it had been lowered into a cavity too small for it; death could well have been brought about by a blow to the head, where a gaping hole in the skull was visible. The remains were carefully removed, subsequent forensic tests establishing them as being male and dating them from about AD40; whoever he was, whatever his race or background, he had been lying there, alone and undiscovered, for nearly two thousand years.

4. A burial-ground for the residents of the Tower once existed to the east of the main buildings but disappeared under the steep approach road to the Tower Bridge when it was built in 1894. However, there are still rooms in the outer eastern wall of the Tower's moat, one of which was believed last used as a morgue after a World War Two enemy spy, Josef Jakobs had been shot by firing squad in the Tower on 15 August 1941.

St Olave's Church, Hart Street.
This church, its gate adorned with five skulls, stands on the corner of Seething Lane and is named after the warlike King of Norway who helped Ethelred against the

Danes. There was a church on this site at least as long ago as 1319, and among the congregation in the 1660s was Samuel Pepys, who as Secretary to the Navy, lived and worked nearby. Samuel's brother Thomas was buried in St Olave's, the famous Diarist noting in his Diary against the date 18 March 1664; 'To church, and with the grave-maker, chose a place for my brother to lie in, just under my mother's pew. But see how a man's tombes are at the mercy of such a fellow, that for sixpence he would, as his own words were "I will justle them together to make room for him", speaking of the fulness of the middle aisle, where he was to lie; and that he would, for my father's sake, do my brother, that is dead, all the civility he can, which was to disturb other corpses that are not so rotten, to make room for him!' In January 1665/6 he wrote 'I presently went into the church. This is the first time I have been there since I left London for the Plague, and it frighted me indeed to go through the church, more than I thought it could have done, to see so many graves lie so high upon the churchyard where people have been buried of the plague. I was much troubled at it, and do not think to go through it again a good while.' The church's register shows that in that parish three hundred and twenty-six victims of the plague were buried there between 4 July and 5 December 1665 . On the 31 January 1666 Pepys wrote that he hoped the churchyard would be covered with lime, and again, on 4 February, when he slinks to church reluctantly, to hear the vicar 'who had been the first to fly (to avoid the Plague) and the last to return', he is much cheered at finding snow covering the dreaded graves.

Newgate Street Churches
Three men had been found guilty and beheaded in 1536 for dallying with a Queen, Anne Boleyn; five years later another rash gentleman succumbed to the regal charms of a lady whose allegiance to her royal husband was not all it might have been, the Queen being Queen Katherine

Howard, Henry VIII's fifth wife. The man involved was her cousin, Thomas Culpepper, his offence being succintly, if medievially described in the *Tyburn Register of Executions* against the date of 10 December 1541, viz. 'At this tyme the Quene, late before (recently) maried to the kyng, called Quene Katheryne, was accused to the Kynge of dissolute liuing ..... and since her Mariage she was vehemently suspected with Thomas Culpepper, who was brought to her Chamber at Lyncolne in Auguste last, by the Lady of Rocheforde (the Queen's Lady-in-Waiting), and were there together alone, from aleuen of the Clocke at Nighte till foure of the Clocke in the Mornyng, and to hym she gaue a Chayne and a rich Cap. Vpon this she was sent to Sion House and there kept close (secure) but yet serued as quene. And for the offence confessed by Culpepper, he was headed, his body buried at Saint Sepulchre's Church by Newgate.' In modern parlance, they met at Court, where Culpepper was highly thought of by Henry VIII; he helped His Majesty to dress, ran errands for him and was at his side for most of the time. As a Gentleman of the King's Privy Council he was a member of the vast entourage accompanying the royal couple as they toured the country, the King's purpose being to show his new bride to the populace, and it was while the party sojourned in Lincoln, York and Pomfret, that Culpepper spent many illicit hours with Katherine, these liaisons being arranged by her Lady-in-Waiting, Jane, Countess Rochford. There is little doubt that the Queen had a deep affection for Culpepper, even to the extent of writing incriminating notes, one saying 'Master Culpepper, I heartily commend myself to you, praying that you send to me word how that you do. I did hear ye were sick and I never longed for anything so much as to see you. Come to me when Lady Rochford be here, for then I shall be best at leisure, to be at your commandment.....trusting to see you again shortly. Yours as long as life endures, Katheryn'. Notes such as these proved to be their Death Warrants; servants talked, the King found out, and the result was inevitable. Cupepper was tried at the Guildhall on 1 December 1541; found guilty, he was decapitated by the axe and, as the *Register* stated, his body was buried in St Sepulchre's Church, Newgate. His head however was utilised in the traditional manner, by being displayed on a pike high on London Bridge as a deterrent, a dire warning to all those passing beneath on their way into the City from the south of the country or the Continent, of what happened to those who dared to have intimate associations with a queen. Before taking its place alongside those who had been executed for other traitorous misdeeds, Culpepper's head was parboiled in salt water and cumin-seed in order to deter the hungry gulls for as long as possible. The Queen herself was beheaded on Tower Green on 13 February 1542 and buried in St Peter's Chapel, as was the conniving Lady Rochford, found guilty for playing a leading part in the illicit liaison. The execution of the latter was poetic justice indeed; she had been the wife of George Rochford, Anne Boleyn's brother, and had given damning evidence against him when he had been accused of adultery and incest with his sister, an offence for which, in May 1536, he too died beneath the axe.

Tower Hill Burial

Hardly a burial ground in a conventional manner, yet the remains of one Miles Syndercombe lie mouldering somewhere beneath the paving stones or roadway of Tower Hill. He was a cashiered quartermaster during the Commonwealth era and, not unlike many others, harboured considerable dislike for the Protector, Oliver Cromwell, but unlike others, he was prepared to convert his dislike into violent action. Employing his military expertise, he constructed a mitrailleuse, an early type of breech-loading machine gun which consisted of no fewer than seven blunderbusses, guns having bell-shaped mouths as muzzles, and arranged to fire simultaneously, their triggers having been being wired together. He mounted this fearsome weapon on a wooden stand inside the window of a house in Hammersmith, on the route along which Cromwell was scheduled to take on his way to Hampton Court. However at the crucial moment, it failed to operate, and Syndercombe resorted to Plan B, that of setting fire to the Chapel of Westminster and murdering Cromwell in the confusion. But a fellow-conspirator informed on him, and on 3 February 1657, before he could finalise the details of his plot, he was arrested, tried, and after having been found guilty of high treason, was incarcerated in the Tower of London, to await his execution.

Desperately he attempted to bribe the yeoman warder guarding him, to help him escape, but on the man's refusal, begged him to obtain poison of some sort. Failing in his attempt to suborn the warder, he then managed to induce his own sister, who was allowed to visit him, to smuggle the necessary drugs into the Tower. On Friday the 13th of February, an appropriate date indeed, he was informed of his manner of death, that on the following morning he would be hanged, drawn and quartered – hanged but cut down while still alive, then disembowelled, beheaded and dismembered. His sister stayed with him until about eight o'clock that evening, and after she had left, Syndercombe asked the now reinforced guard of five yeoman warders to leave him along for a while so that he could pray. The guards considerately left the room, and later reported that when he opened the door to them shortly afterwards, he was 'rubbing his hands together and then about his mouth and nose', and heard him exclaim "I have done, and pray you to come in!" Presently he undressed and, getting into bed, drew the curtains around it. A few minutes later the warders heard a snorting noise and on pulling the curtains back, found their prisoner had taken poison and was on the point of death. Although every effort was made to resuscitate him, he passed away at midnight.

He had left a note stating that he had killed himself, not to escape the suffering of execution, but to avoid the disgrace of a felon's death, and this was read out to the coroner's jury, meeting in the Tower, who brought in a verdict of death by poisoning. But there was no Christian burial for Miles Syndercombe, for the Law hates being cheated of its due prey, and on 17 February 1657 his disfigured corpse was tied to a horse's tail and dragged up the slope to Tower Hill where 'a hole being digged, he was turned in, stark naked, and a stake spiked with iron was driven through him into the earth; that part of the stake which remains above ground being all plated with iron, which may stand as an example of terror to all traitors for all time to come.'

Chapter 6 – Dissenters' Burial-grounds
Everlasting coffins

Because body snatchers could easily break open wooden coffins, some firms manufactured and sold iron or lead ones. One advertisement appeared in *Wooler's British Gazette* on 13 October 1822, announcing; 'Many hundred dead bodies will be dragged from their wooden coffins this winter for the anatomical lectures which have just commenced, for the articulators, and for those who deal in the dead, for the supply of country practitioners and the Scotch schools. The violation of the sanctity of the grave is said to be needful for the instruction of the medical pupil, but let each one about to inter a mother, husband, child or friend, say to themselves, shall I devote the object of my affection to such a purpose; if not, the only safe coffin is Bridgman's Patent wrought-iron one, charged the same price as a wooden one, and is a superior substitute for lead. Edward Lillie Bridgman of 34 Fish Street Hill and Goswell Street Road, performs funerals in any part of the Kingdom and by attention to moderate charges insures the recommendation of those who employ him.' Lead coffins were also on the market, the lids of which were then soldered down, and the same effect was achieved in the Bridgman version, it having interior spring catches which locked when the lid was placed in position. Eventually however, it was realised by the church authorities that, unlike the wooden versions, these would never rot away, and the result would be cemeteries packed full with metal containers for many centuries to come.

Chapter 7 – Burial-grounds of Foreigners in London

Theodore, King of Corsica

Holding the title of Baron von Neuhoff, Theodore Etienne was born in Metz about 1696, the son of a Westphalian gentleman of good family; he served with the French Army and, later becoming a member of the Swedish diplomatic service, he made the acquaintance of some Corsican insurgents who were endeavouring to free their country from Genoese rule. The Baron obtained some ammunition and financial backing from the Bey of Tunis in exchange for a promise of a monopoly of trade with a 'free' Corsica, plus a port being made available for the Bey's pirate ships, and he arrived in Corsica in 1736. Having achieved their independence, the Corsicans proceeded to elect him King, with full powers to establish a mint and award honours and orders of knighthood. However his popularity soon waned, and he later left the island and travelled round Europe, seeking further supplies of arms with which he could re-ingratiate himself with the Corsicans and thereby regain his throne. Some years later, having purchased a shipload of armaments, he returned, only to find that the French were supporting the Genoese and the insurgents were being overwhelmed.

Dispirited and penniless he went into exile in London, Horace Walpole, Earl of Orford taking him under his wing to the extent that, when Theodore was imprisoned in the King's Bench Prison for debt, Walpole managed to secure his release. Shortly afterwards, however, he fell sick, and died on 11 December 1756. A 'pauper's grave' seemed inevitable until a certain John Wright, described as 'an oilman living in Compton Street, Soho', came forward and declared that "he, for once, would pay the funeral expenses of a King!" Accordingly His Late Majesty was interred in St Ann's graveyard, the minister at first refusing to allow Walpole to have a tombstone inscribed 'King of Corsica' erected there, but he later relented, and an inscription, beneath a crown copied from a Corsican coin, bore the words 'Near this place is interred THEODORE, KING OF CORSICA, who died in this parish December 11, 1756, immediately after leaving the King's Bench Prison, by the Act of Insolvency; in Consequence of which he registerd the Kingdom of Greece for the Use of his Creditors.'

Chapter 8 – Hospital, Almshouse and Workhouse Grounds
Southwark Bridge Road
To demonstrate the fate of the original burial-ground of the St Saviour's Workhouse, the caption beneath an illustration in the Queen's London, published in 1896, states 'In Southwark Bridge Road are the Headquarters of the Metropolitan Fire Brigade, marked by a large tower, from the summit of which a constant watch is kept. The Brigade, established in 1866, is maintained at an annual cost of £130,000 per annum, and the area which it protects extends over 118 square miles. In the course of a year some 5000 alarms, of which, however, a large proportion are false, are given, and from thirty to forty million gallons of water are used in extinguishing fires.'

Chapter 9 – Private Cemeteries
Tyburn
Following the Restoration of Charles II to the throne, retribution was carried out on three of the men who had sentenced his father, Charles I, to death; although Oliver Cromwell, his son-in-law Henry Ireton, and Lord President of the Court, John Bradshaw, had all died, their corpses were disinterred from Westminster Abbey and, to quote an account written by Sir George Wharton in 1662 'The odious carcases of O. Cromwell, H. Ireton and J. Bradshaw were drawn upon sledges to Tyburn on the anniversary of the execution of Charles I and, being pulled out of their Coffins, there hanged on the several angles of

the Triple Tree till Sunset. Then taken down, beheaded, and their loathsome Truncks thrown into a deep hole beneath the gallows. Their heads were afterwards set up on Poles on the top of Westminster Hall.'

The Times of 9 May 1860 reported that during excavations on the site in Edgeware Road, workmen uncovered a quantity of bones, obviously the remains of some of those who had been hanged there. Since the cadavers of most victims were taken away, either for dissection or display as deterrents, it is possible that those unearthed could have been the remains of the three Roundhead leaders.

It has been estimated that during its six hundred years existence, over 50,000 people, both men and women, were executed at Tyburn. The exact position of the scaffold is impossible to determine, since from 1759 it ceased to be a fixture, but was assembled whenever it was required, not always occupying the same place. Even in those days, NIMBY, 'not in my back yard', was an ever-present factor, the *Gazetteer* of 4 May 1771 stating 'The Dowager Lady Waldegrave is having a grand house built near Tyburn, and through the particular interest of her Ladyship, the place of execution will be moved to another spot.' It would certainly seem, however, to have been originally positioned at or near the junction of Edgeware Road (Watling Street) and Oxford Street/Baywater Road, adjacent to Marble Arch. At that junction is a small traffic island bearing a symbolic plaque bearing the words 'Here Stood Tyburn Tree, Removed 1759'. In 1571 the standard type of gallows, two posts and a cross-piece, was improved, another post and two further cross-pieces being added, to increase the through-put of victims from seven at a time to twenty-one; its new configuration then became known as the Triple Tree.

Although the original names of surrounding streets, Tyburn Way, Tyburn Road, etc., have been changed to the more socially-acceptable ones of the present-day, the old name of Tyburn still survives in that of the nearby Tyburn Convent, a lasting reminder of the 105 Carthusians,

Benedictines, Jesuits and many others who, between 1535 and 1681, lost their lives on the scaffold; some of its ancient timbers, together with other holy relics, are still revered by the Tyburn nuns there.

Chapter 12 – Cemeteries still in Use

Lavish funeral expenses

Mrs Holmes deplored the unnecessary extravagance of Victorian funerals, and rightly so. The social mores of the day had to be strictly observed, and no expense was spared when it came to the death of a loved one, no convention ignored, no detail excluded. The wearing of black clothes by everyone concerned was de rigeur; where applicable, front doors bore a hatchment, a diamond-shaped tablet bearing the diseased' coat-of-arms, the door knockers being swathed with ribbon, a black one if the deceased had been married or aged, a white ribbon if young or single. A mute dressed in black had to be employed to stand on funereal duty outside the door, and the corpse was laid out in a darkened room, the only illumination being provided by wax candles mounted in wall sconces, barely sufficient for mourners to take a last look at the face of the deceased. Gifts of black gloves, scarves and mourning rings had to be purchased, to present to mourning relatives and close family friends, and a splendid meal, almost a banquet, had to be provided at the appropriate time. The hearses and horses were adorned with great plumes of ostrich feathers, the animals having black saddle cloths, and should the funeral take place at night, the cortege was escorted by a large retinue bearing torches.

Yet despite all the plumes and pomp, the black-edged handkerchiefs and visiting cards, by the end of that century, many of the corpses of 'the late lamented and dearly missed' finished up beneath a builder's yard or children's playground – and by the end of the twentieth century, had been concreted over as part of the foundations of busy streets and modern housing estates.'

Appendix A – Burial Grounds which still Exist

The Priory of Bermondsey (Appendix A, No. 228)

Queen Catherine de Valois, was the consort of Henry V, who died in 1422. Some time later, at a palace ball, her Clerk to the Wardrobe, a handsome young man named Owen Tudor, happened to overbalance while attempting an intricate pirouette, and ended up with his head in the Queen's lap. This intimate, albeit accidental meeting, fostered a closer relationship between them, and they secretly married sometime about 1425, and had five chidren. Ultimately court and parliament opposition forced them to separate, and Owen was later imprisoned in both Newgate Gaol and the Tower of London before being eventually freed. He subsequently became a captain in the Lancastrian army during the War of Roses, during which, he was captured, and sentenced to death at Hereford. On the scaffold he exclaimed "This head shall lie on the block that was wont to lie on Queen Catherine's lap!" After being decapitated, his remains were buried within the Priory of Grey Friars, Hereford. It is little realised that Owen Tudor was the founder of the Tudor dynasty, for Edmund, his eldest son by Catherine, became the father of Henry VII, the family line continuing through Henry VIII and Queens Mary and Elizabeth!

Misfortune and tragedy also overtook Owen's wife, Catherine of Valois. Finding herself alone and husbandless, in 1436, aged only thirty-six, she retreated from social life and took up royal lodgings in Bermondsey Priory, its site now but a small plot of land next to where the internationally renowned weekly antique market is held. Sadly, she died a year later, and her corpse was taken to the Lady Chapel in Westminster Abbey, but instead of being buried, her coffin was partially wrapped in a sheet of lead from the Abbey roof and, the lid not having been replaced, her body was exposed from the waist upwards, it becoming a macabre tourist attraction to see and touch her parched corpse. As described by the historian John Dart (d.1730) 'the bones being firmly united and thinly covered with flesh, like the scrapings of fine leather.' It remained on public view for over two hundred and thirty years, Samuel Pepys joining the queue and later exulting in his *Diary* that 'On Shrove Tuesday 1669 I to the Abbey went, and by favour, did see the body of Queen Katherine of Valois, and had the upper part of her body in my hands, and I did kiss her mouth, reflecting that I did kiss a queen; and this my birthday, and I thirty-six years old, and I did kiss a Queen!' It was not until 1776 that decency eventually prevailed, and Catherine de Valois was reverently interred in the Abbey's vaults.

Burned Church (Appendix A, No. 278 and subsequent similar entries);
These were the results of the Great Fire of London which started on 12 September 1666, during which no fewer than eighty churches and twelve thousand houses were destroyed. An excerpt from the *Diary* written by eye-witness John Evelyn (1620-1706) read: 'the whole neighbourhood by the Thames was burnt out as far as Baynard's Castle. On the north the fire spread as far as Gracechurch Street, Lombard Street, Cornhill and Bucklersbury, and so caught the houses built about the Exchange. Before Tuesday's dawn the Exchange and other buildings in the neighbourhood were burnt. By that night the flames had spread to Fleet Street, and had burnt all the houses as far as St Dunstan's Church, together with all the buildings lying between the Exchange and the Temple, Crown Court, etc., the whole sweep of which was consumed by the fire, which then deviated from its direct course and turned up Fetter Lane, about half-way towards Holborn. Thus it lasted until Wednesday night. Then a fresh fire broke out in the Temple, and was got under control by about two o'clock Thursday morning, when it had destroyed buildings about the cloisters and ignited a portion of the church and the hall. By Thursday the fire had, for the most part, been overcome – at Temple Church. near Holborn Bridge, at Pie Corner, Aldersgate,

Cripplegate, the lower end of Coleman Street, the end of Basinghall Street, the gates at Bishopsgate Street and Fall Street, the Standard at Cornhill, the church in Fenchurch Street, Clothworkers' Hall in Mincing Lane, the middle of Mark Lane and the Tower Dock. Here the conflagration came to an end, after the fire had burnt out and destroyed the largest and best part of the City, where most of the merchants lived. In an hour's walk, from the Temple to the Tower, there is, within the walls, hardly anything left standing; and outside the walls, in Fleet Street and from Holborn to Fleet Bridge, all is in ruins.'

St Botolph's Church, Aldgate (Appendix A, No. 281):
Although not actually the churchyard itself, the ground beneath the steps fronting the church became the repository of human remains, namely the head of Henry Grey, Duke of Suffolk, 3rd. Marquis of Dorset, Privy Councillor – and father of Queen Jane, better known as Lady Jane Grey. When Mary became Queen, Henry Grey took part in a campaign against her intentions to marry Philip of Spain, an alliance which would reinforce the Roman Catholic Queen in her efforts to eliminate the nation's Protestantism. Captured in an attempt to seize Coventry on 30 January 1553/4, he was tried and sentenced to death for high treason. A few days after his daughter's execution within the walls of the Tower of London, he was taken to Tower Hill and there, before a vast crowd, presented his gown and doublet to the executioner, and, as was the custom, forgave the man, saying "God forgive thee, and I do" adding, "And when thou doest thine office, I pray thee do it quickly, and God have mercy to thee." However, nervous or inefficient, the executioner needed to deliver two blows with the axe to sever the ducal head.

By some means, the head was retrieved by the family and buried in the vault of the family chapel, part of their mansion situated in the Minories, adjacent to the Tower. Many decades later the building was demolished and replaced by the Church of the Holy Trinity. In 1852 the vault was entered by Lord Dartmouth and the head retrieved. As described in *Six Hundred Years of Historical Sketches of Eminent Men and Women who have more or less come into contact with the Abbey and Church of Holy Trinity, Minories, from 1293-1893* by the Rev. Samuel Kinnes, published in 1898; Lord Dartmouth came across something which might have been a basket full of sawdust, but on examining it, found it to contain a head in a most remarkable state of preservation. I think it was most probable that it was oaken sawdust which, acting as a disinfectant, had not only preserved the head from decay, but had so mummified it that the features have remained sufficiently perfect for anyone acquainted with the Duke's likeness to recognise him...........and I think it possible that if the sawdust was of oak, it would really tan the skin of the face to leather in the most natural way possible. The hair of the head came away with the sawdust and the basket was quite perished.'

The Church of Holy Trinity ceased to be a place of worship in 1899 and, despite a bid being made by an American collector who offered £500 for the relic, it was transferred to the neighbouring St Botolph's Church, Aldgate, where, earlier in the twentieth century, the vicar would give the morbidly curious visitor the opportunity to view the mummified head in its glass container. One who surveyed it was Major-General Sir George Younghusband, Keeper of the Jewel House, Tower of London, who afterwards described it in some detail; 'There is no shrinkage of the face, the eyes are wide open and the eye balls and pupils perfectly preserved, though of a parchment colour. The skin, too, all over is of the same yellowish hue. When found, the hair of the head and the beard were still on, but owing to its very brittle state and from having been handled by several people, these broke off, though in a strong light the bristles may still be seen. The nose is not quite perfect, but the ears are practically as in life. The head had evidently been severed by two heavy blows, and loose skin, jagged and

Newgate Prison: The "Graveyard" looking towards the door leading to the Old Bailey

looking like loose parchment, demonstrates where the severence occurred.' Some half century or more later, Christian respect for the grim relic was finally shown, and it was interred beneath the paving stones at the church's entrance.

Newgate Burial-ground (Appendix A, No.364)
After the hanged victims had been cut down and the inquest completed, they were buried in quick-lime in the prison cemetery, a narrow passage connecting the prison to the Old Bailey, through which the prisoners passed to and from their trial. The only visible record of burial was a single initial cut in the wall. The passage was open to the air but was covered with an iron grating, and was known among the prisoners as 'Birdcage Walk.'

St Dunstan's in the East (Appendix A, No. 381)
This church was badly damaged during the Great Fire of 1666, Sir Christopher Wren designing its reconstruction.

While digging the foundations the workmen found immense walls of chalk and rubble stretching in all directions where the early monks were supposed to have dwelt, and also discovered a bricked-up porch leading into a bone-house, a storage area for the skeletal parts after the coffins and flesh had crumbled away and disintegrated.

SELECT BIBLIOGRAPHY

Abbott, G. *Book Of Execution*, Headline, 1994

Bayne-Powell, R. *Eighteenth Century London Life*, Murray, 1932

Bell, WG, *London Rediscoveries*, Bodley Head, 1929

Camm, Dom Bede. *Forgotten Shrines*, Macdonald and Evans, 1910

Davey, R. *Pageant of London*, Methuen, 1906

Gentlemen's Magazine – Various

Gordon, C. *Old Bailey and Newgate*, Fisher Unwin, 1902

Holmes, B. *London Burial Grounds*, Fisher Unwin, 1901

Ivimey, A. *History of London*, Sampson, Low, 1932

John O' London, *London Stories*, Newnes, 1910

Lang, A. *Social England Illustrated*, Constable, 1903

Ogden, M. *In Search of Cemeteries*, private pub. 1922

Stow, J. *Survey of London*, 1912

Taylor, G. *Historical Guide to London*, Dent, 1911

The Queen's London, Cassell, 1896

Thornbury, W. *Old and New London*, 1874

Timbs, J. *Romance of London*, Warne, 1865

Tower of London Records

STREET INDEX

All streets mentioned in the book are listed here; those renamed/ demolished are also included as evidence of their earlier existence and location.